The Binman's Guide to Selling
Top 100 selling techniques, words, strategies, tips, scripts & inspirations

Oisín Browne

The Binman's Guide to Selling: *Top 100 selling techniques, words, strategies, tips, scripts & inspirations*

Copyright 2013 © Oisín Browne
All rights reserved.

This edition is published by Drop The Monkey Publishing.
For further information: www.dropthemonkey.com

Published in the Republic of Ireland
Printed by Gemini International
Cover Design by Links Associates

First Edition

ISBN 978-0-9570130-1-8

A catalogue record for this book is available from the British Library.

This publication is designed to provide accurate and authoritative information in regard to the subject matter covered. It is sold with the understanding that the publisher is not engaged in rendering legal services or other professional services. If legal advice or other expert assistance is required, the services of a competent professional person should be sought.

The author and publisher state that all writings in this book are the suggestions and views of the author and accept no responsibility for the outcome of any suggestions applied.

To buy **The Binman's Guide To Selling** in bulk contact the publisher at info@dropthemonkey.com - The book is ideal for your management team or as a corporate gift for your clients, suppliers or partners. Special discounts are available on quantity purchases by corporations, associations, businesses, networking groups, universities, business schools, sales teams, agencies, and for seminars.

Praise for The Binman's Guide to Selling

"Words matter!! And Browne's book provides the precise language and approaches to ramp-up your sales effectiveness – one bite-sized piece at a time. Commit 60 seconds per day to read one tip and apply it and experience the positive impact it has on your sales." *Verne Harnish, Founder, Entrepreneurs' Organization and author of 'Mastering the Rockefeller Habits'*

"As a coach for executives and entrepreneurs worldwide, I have found that most people dread selling. Oisín Browne has transformed the "I hate to sell" mindset into a joyful process of sharing what you love. With 100 insightful terms and tips, he gives us an entire language to get our customers excited about our business" *Libby Gill, Business Coach and Bestselling Author of 'You Unstuck'*

"This cool little book on selling is fast and fun. If you make your living selling, and just one tip makes you money, then the book is worth ten times its price." *Jeffrey J.Fox, author of the international best seller, 'How To Become a Rainmaker', selected as one of the hundred best business books ever written*

"Oisín Browne has created an invaluable reference tool for salespeople and sales teams in this book. Want to tap into the customer's desire? Browne's book is destined to become a necessary tool in any salesperson's arsenal". *Marshall Goldsmith, million-selling author of the New York Times bestsellers, MOJO and What Got You Here Won't Get You There*

"This is a book that puts everything together… solid advice from the real world of sales and business." *Steve Schiffman, leading motivational speaker, sales trainer and author of over 50 sales and business development books*

"A dictionary of simple thoughts that can make a profound difference in your selling approach." *Al Ries, bestselling author of 'War in the Boardroom' and 'Positioning: The Battle for Your Mind'*

"Without people who sell the products and the services that we all need, the world of commerce would grind to a halt. We need salespeople. Selling is a honourable profession. Want to be great at selling? Well, this little book has more useful tips than you could ever need!" *Dr. Paddi Lund, author of 'Building the Happiness-Centred Business'*

Contents

Selling Techniques,
Strategies, Tips, Scripts & Inspirations

Bonus Chapter

FOREWORD

Want to be top at selling? This little book has far more useful tips than you could ever need!

Without people who sell the products and the services that we all need, the world of commerce would grind to a halt. We need salespeople. Selling is a honourable profession. Between these two covers, you will find information that has taken years to accumulate. All of the ideas are winners. But I would caution you not to try to use all of them... there are just too many... you would go crazy!

Pick the ones that ring a bell with you, that fit with your character and inclinations. Then it is important to integrate these techniques into your personality, so that they become a part of you and all that you do in your chosen profession.

Most people like to buy, but do not like to feel that they are being 'sold to'. So your words and actions when you use these new ideas need to become seamless. Then, as you progress, you will find that you are not really selling at all; you are merely helping your customer to buy. You have become that most enviable of professionals: a 'buyer's adviser'.

Perhaps Oisín won't mind if I add one tip of my own: *'Do not be too hungry for a sale'*. In my opinion, selling goes best when you do not really need a particular sale. If you are desperate you will push too hard and may even violate your own ethics by exaggerating or distorting the truth. Then, at best you will lose the sale because your customer will feel pressured and at worst you will get the sale but feel guilty because it was not in your customer's best interest to buy.

So live within your means and you can relax with your customer, and chat together, and learn about each other and talk together, and just enjoy one another's company. For in the end, that's what selling is all about: helping your customer to be happy. And strangely enough, if you make your customers happier they will buy more readily and your work will be more enjoyable … and your life will become happier. Wonderful stuff this selling!

Dr. Paddi Lund, *author of 'Building the Happiness-Centred Business'*

PREFACE

I believe we are all born sales people. As a child, you went into selling mode the very first time you placed all your efforts into convincing your parents to buy the toy you saw in the television advert. You were in selling mode when you asked your first love out on a date. Everybody sells everyday without even knowing that they are using their selling skills. The actor sells their acting abilities when they are looking to get the leading role in a film. You sell the idea that the meal will be more tasty and satisfying when persuading your partner to go for the pizza over the healthy salad. When choosing where to go on holiday you sell the idea to yourself that one place is going to be better than another. You sell the idea that you are the person for the position when you go for a job interview. In every action we sell, be it to ourselves or to others.

I would have never dreamt that I would learn the best lessons in the business of selling from the back of a bin truck. That is exactly what I did when I started working and collecting the waste on the commercial route at The City Bin Co. Working on the truck was a kin to the classroom. I was always learning; I was learning about time management when I would be starting anywhere between 3 and 6 in the morning. I worked hard in all conditions to get the job done. I learned the invaluable daily tutorial of teamwork. I was exercising everyday and keeping myself fit without even knowing it. Eight hours a day running after a big truck and picking up trash tends to do that. This taught me that when your body is fit your mind is more focused. These small actions were shaping the foundation for my career in business and sales. On the bin truck, there was the driver, the helper and yours truly, the second helper. Each of us pulled our weight. Getting up early, I quickly learned the value of having a routine and being responsible for that timetable and the daily tasks.

When I first started, I was giving a hand to my brother, the CEO and Co-founder of The City Bin Co., Gene. The company was in its infancy but had sights on rapid expansion and growth. I felt that I had a huge part to play in the development and success of the company. Gene would ask me to help out at the weekends. Little did I know that 15 years on I would be working for the same company, playing an integral role shaping the sales strategy for the different markets. I have seen the company grow from a hand full of employees with one truck, two customers and four bins in one city to well over 100 staff with a full fleet of trucks stretching from the west coast to the east coast of Ireland.

I wasn't just collecting the waste containers. Working with a large household and business customer base I found myself in the heart of the selling and customer service world. I was speaking to the customers. I got to know the customers, their businesses and their stories. They got to know me. I was going the extra mile for the customers. I was building relationships with the customers and I was always looking for new leads to convert to customers. From door knocking, cold calling, warm leads and meetings, I found myself in the core of the business-to-business and business-to-customer world. Through these real life business experiences, this is where I learned the ropes of selling.

After four years on the bin truck, I moved to the office to be at the coalface of the sales department. This is where I got my first taste of working in the customer centre. I was answering calls and helping with the accounts department. Before long, I was back on the road, but this time I was delivering the products, meeting the customers and I was signing up new leads. I was selling. I wasn't selling skips or bin bags. I was selling excellent customer service. I was learning the ups and downs of winning and losing customers. I wanted to understand the reasons behind customer loyalty, customer churn and customers who would re-engage. I was learning the importance of customer retention and the value of what I was selling to both the customer and the company.

I joined business-networking groups where I represented the company and showcased the services that I was selling. It was a great place to make new connections and get referrals. I learned how to speak and present products in public at these meetings. In 2011, I co-founded a local business network called the Business Motivation Group, a business support group that offers motivational talks, support, and inspirations to businesses.

Today, I am a shareholder in The City Bin Co., working closely with the sales and marketing teams. I am proud to be part of a business where the learning is endless and my growing never stops. I am a student when it comes to selling. I am always learning and eager to learn more. This book, The Binman's Guide to Selling is my '*Top 100 Selling Techniques*' that I have collected, learned and used throughout my selling experiences. My one wish is to keep learning, keep having experiences and keep sharing these lessons.

Oisín Browne

INTRODUCTION

Selling waste collection services brings one in contact with many diverse people and businesses - from single dwelling homes to large multinationals. The Irish waste collection industry is unique as every individual home and business is free to choose it's own waste collection company. To grow a waste collection business in Ireland you need to be good at marketing, selling, innovating and good old fashioned customer service.

The Binman's Guide to Selling compiles the learning from selling across this diverse customer base into a single book. It's not about the waste industry though. The business just happens to be in the waste collection sector. These principles and techniques apply across every sector; they are universal.

In 2008 Ireland experienced one of the most rapid economic declines in post World War II Europe. As I write this in 2013, the country is still waiting on signs of recovery. However, during this crisis, while the domestic economy shrunk 25% and prices fell across all sectors, The City Bin Co. experienced 18% compound sales growth. You can say that The City Bin Co. has a sales culture.

For the past 15 years Oisin has been representing the company on many different fronts, working on the trucks, in the office, in the customer centre, on the marketing team and working directly in sales. Regardless of the position he has always been selling. Selling the company's service, reputation, the brand, products as well as building relationships. Every employee is selling, all of the time, whether they know it or not.

The Binman's Guide to Selling has captured this fifteen years of learning from across the different business areas. It is a unique collection of tips, tools and actions to increase success in both the sales field and beyond. I hope you enjoy it and benefit from the learning inside.

Gene Browne, *CEO of The City Bin Co.*

GET THE BEST FROM THIS BOOK

When you get an idea from this book that you believe would be beneficial to you or your company, set the wheels in motion by putting it to use. Make it yours. Maybe it is a technique that you already practice. Bring that selling skill to a new level.

The simple goal of this little book is to stimulate, motivate, and to inspire you to be creative, innovative and professional when selling. As a business owner or sales person, this will allow your products and services to be seen in the most advantageous light by the potential customer. We all know that you must meet your targets. We all know how difficult that can be in the dog eat dog world of selling. The big questions are: How can you achieve outstanding results in your field? What will give you the edge over your competitor? What will make you and what you are selling irresistible? What will make you a great sales person? Great sales people know that selling is all in the mind. This book will help you develop the extraordinary selling skills you need to have a winning sales mindset. Above all, it will help you to get inside the minds of your potential customers, giving you the power to correctly educate them about the value of your product, influence their decisions and reassure them that you can get the job done.

This collection of selling suggestions is for those with an interest in business and sales. It is for the person starting to study business and sales. It is for the sales person who has just started a career in selling. It is for the sales and management teams of small, medium and big companies. It is also for the curious person who studies at the University of Life and wishes to add a little more to their ever-increasing pool of knowledge. In fact, no business student or selling professional should be without it.

Building strong customer relationships with existing clients is essential in winning future sales. You will learn how to make life long connections with potential customers and you will be inspired to find more creative, innovative ways of selling to them. No prospect wants to be pressured into buying. They want to be in a relaxed environment where they can be educated about your product. They want to make the decision themselves. To guide them to a desirable outcome, you must be clear about what you want from the sale before you meet your customers. This will enable you to display your products and services in the best possible light and to focus on the customer. To do this, you need to tune yourself into their needs. Most importantly, you need to close the sale!

These chapters are designed to be short and sweet and easy to flick through. There is not so much information that you will go astray, yet there are enough techniques, words, strategies, interviews, scripts and tips to keep you hooked.

This book is written to encourage creative thinking that can be applied when selling. No matter what stage you are at in your selling career, it is always helpful to have some food for thought. This is your book, so be sure to write on it, add to it and highlight the parts that you find interesting and useful.

This is not a novel. To get the best from this guide, do not read it from the front cover to the back cover. Read it from the back cover to the front cover. To get the greatest benefit from this book, leave it in your favourite reading place, be this a coffee table, a bedside locker, your car, your office desk or the bathroom. The book is written in a way that allows you to randomly open it at any point and start reading at any particular page you choose. Enjoy the read and give yourself a good dose of inspiration!

Advanced Selling Suggestions & Word Psychology Techniques

What you say and how you say it can break or make the deal depending on your choice of words. The right words can have a powerful impact on directing the sale towards the desired positive outcome. They give you greater confidence to deliver the sale. They encourage potential customers to look at your products and services in a new way.

There is a common thread between all of the words in this section. They act as markers, guiding you through the sales process. If you lose control of the conversation, they give you the power to bring the meeting back to the selling zone where you can reconnect, take charge and communicate a course of action that allows you to close the sale.

Each word will have a slightly different impact when speaking with potential customers. Some words are used to make an emotional connection with the potential customer's past positive buying experiences. Some are a call to action. Some act as a means to refocus the conversation, while others are red flags that enable you to qualify the direction and stage of the sale.

Context is everything. If you use a word in a positive context, you will create a positive image in the potential customer's mind. Sometimes a natural alternative will arise and sometimes you can combine them with other phrases to increase their effectiveness. You will instinctively be drawn to some words more than others. The important thing is to choose words that feel comfortable for you, so you will sound natural and sincere when you say them.

Your goal is to relax and to help the potential customer relax, focus and connect with you and what you are selling. When people are relaxed, they are more open to suggestion. When they are focused they will make decisions and when they are connected with you, rapport is built and opportunity to do business is born. This creates an opening for you to educate the potential customer on what you have to offer and show them that your offering is different. Use this collection of words as a reference point when delivering your sales pitch. Take them and make them yours.

1. IMAGINE

How it Works

When you ask a potential client to imagine, you are asking them to create a mental image. You are guiding them to that magic feeling that they will have from the benefit of using your product. This gives them a sense of ownership.

Making a suggestion to imagine allows them to paint a picture of themselves with your product while tapping into a very positive feeling. They will begin to feel that they are already using your product in a way that works for them, which creates an emotional connection with the image in their mind and your brand. Keep it simple and allow them to fill in the gaps. Another good alternative to the word '*Imagine*' is to say, '*See Yourself*'.

What to Say

'Now **imagine**, *for a moment, sitting in this car and cruising down the main street. **Imagine** the people looking at you and thinking WOW, I wish I was like him. That would be great, wouldn't it?'*

You can also say, '***Imagine** using this product for two months. **Imagine** how great you would feel, to be able to fit into your jeans comfortably. Being able to exercise without running out of breath and best of all, could you **imagine** all that extra energy you would have? Wouldn't it be great?'*

Imagine is a great word to use when a potential client gives you an objection in relation to price. A prospect tells you at the end of your pitch: *"You know, I just can't afford it."* You can reply, *"That's fair enough, I understand. But **imagine** for a moment that you could afford it. Would you be happy to come on board right away?"*

If the potential client agrees and replies, *"Yes, of course"* you can then suggest working on a price plan that would suit both you and the potential client.

2. BASED ON WHAT YOU TOLD ME

How it Works

A nice way to summarise your product while giving credit to the customer is to compliment them on their decision. You retain your control and position as expert on the service or product that you are selling.

It is important to establish an emotional connection while conveying empathy for the experience they have had. You demonstrate to the potential customer that you are listening and understand what they need when you lead with *'Based on what you told me.'* It links and connects the conversation to what you can offer bringing your prospect a step closer to closing.

What to Say

*'**Based on what you have told me**, here's what I would recommend for you. I would recommend X, Y and Z because you will save money, and time, and be free of stress. Are you happy to go with that?'*

*'**Based on what you told me**, the next step for us would be X, Y and Z. Would you agree?'*

It is also a great leading phrase that can help your potential client to choose.

*'**Based on what you have told me,** I believe it is fair to say that you already know what you want. How would you make this product work best for you?'*

It is saying to the potential client: you made the decision and you will make the savings.

*'James, **based on what you have told me**, it really looks like you could see some significant savings with our product. Wouldn't that be great?'*

3. IMPOSSIBLE/POSSIBLE

How it Works

These are reinforcement words that carry no doubt. They are opposite sides of the same coin. Although *'impossible'* alone means that something cannot be done, it delivers a strong punch when used creatively. The word *'possible'* on the other hand, is great when you are asking for the business. It eliminates the *'no'* option, as everything is possible.

What to Say

*'It will be **impossible** for you not to love this dress.'*

*'It would be **impossible** to find a better deal.'*

It is not uncommon to hear a hypnotherapist say to his client who wishes to stop smoking:

*'It will be **impossible** for you to hold a cigarette in your hand and it will be even more **impossible** for you to put a cigarette in your mouth just as you will find it **impossible** to put it in your hand in the first place.'*

If a potential client is giving you an objection, you could say:

*'You know John, I believe nothing is **impossible**, so what would it take for you and me to do business here today?'*

At the end of a meeting, when you are asking for the business or scheduling a follow up meeting:

*'I think our conversation today was really productive. Is it **possible** for us to do business together?'*

*'I am free next Monday afternoon. Is it **possible** to have a follow up meeting with you?'*

4. WALK THROUGH

How it Works

It is so important to make the prospect comfortable with the details of the product that you are presenting. You know what you are selling inside out because you work with it every day, but the prospect is meeting you and getting information on what you sell for the first time.

Before you offer anything, tell the prospect that you will guide them through the process. You want the prospect to feel relaxed and reassured. One-way to achieve this is to tell them what you will do before you do it. This can qualify the stage of the sale, remove any doubt from their mind and give clarity to the prospect, allowing them concentrate on the agenda. Let them know that you will *'walk through'* the different options with them. Clearly show them their options, so they have all the information needed to make their decision. This displays to the prospect that you know what you are talking about.

What to Say

Tell the prospect exactly why you are with them and what steps you are going to take. This lets them know that you are confident and knowledgeable about what you sell. This builds trust. You can influence the outcome of the sale when the prospect has trust in you.

*'Let me **walk through** the various packages on offer. Together we will be able to find you one that fits.'*

Reconfirm the prospect's interest in you and your product by saying:

*'John, I am interested in moving forward with this project. Are you available for a call on Monday to **walk through** everything?'*

5. RECOMMEND

How it Works

To recommend something is to endorse, suggest or speak well of a product or service to the potential customer. *'Recommend'* is a word that advocates what you are selling, once trust has been created between you and the prospect. It shows that you are an expert who is educated in the products and services that you sell.

What to Say

To recommend is to give direction without being too pushy. After delivering your pitch, you may say to your potential client:

'From the three different products I have shown you today, I highly **recommend** *this product, which is low cost, time saving and has many of the same features as the other two products. Would you be happy to go with that?'*

After the prospect has happily committed to the purchase of your product or service, you can always ask:

'Can you **recommend** *any of your neighbours that may be interested in products like the one you just purchased?'*

If the prospect suggests somebody, you can say directly to that person:

'I just signed up a new client who is a neighbour of yours and he **recommended** *that I speak to you. Are you interested in saving some money and time like your neighbour?'*

'*Recommend*' can also be used as a third party testimonial when speaking to a prospect.

'Joe from the next street has been using this product for the last two years. He **recommends** *it to everybody and he doesn't even work with me. He is so happy that he saved money and time he tells me that sharing is caring and caring is a great feeling. Would you like to have that same great feeling that Joe has?'*

6. YOU

How it Works

You should always have more '*you*' than '*I*' in your pitch. To you it may appear that it is all about the product, but the truth is, without customers, your product has no meaning. It is about the potential client and tapping into their desire to make a purchase on a given day, in a given place. It is about how it will benefit them. It opens up a dialogue, so you can find out more about their business. '*You*' is a warm, inclusive word, which shows the prospect that you are focused on them.

What to Say

Instead of saying to the prospect "*This system is easy to operate. I have tested it myself,*" you can say "***You** will be surprised how safe and easy this system is to operate.*"

Make it personal and about the client. Don't say

'*I can see this as a good fit for your business*'.

Prepare the prospect to get into ownership mode.

'*James, how do **you** envision what is on offer here as a good fit for your business?*'

This encourages dialogue towards a positive decision in favour of your product or service.

7. UNDERSTAND

How it Works

To say *'I understand'* to a potential customer or existing client is to acknowledge and appreciate their situation. When a customer explains their position to you and you respond with "I understand," it shows that you are listening and that you care. It is important that the sales person has great empathy with the prospect and their situation in order to build trust, rapport and have success. You relate to the prospect in a way that creates a level of trust and understanding.

You are letting the prospect know that you have the ability to sense, feel, understand and react to their purchasing needs. You are creating a rapport with the potential customer, which builds trust and which ultimately places you a step closer to achieving success with the sale.

What to Say

When you say *'I **understand**,'* you tap into the emotions of the person to whom you are selling.

*'I **understand**. If I were in your shoes, I would be saying exactly the same thing you are saying right now.'*

*'My only goal today is to give you the most up to date information so that you **understand** the workings of our service and how it can benefit you and your business.'*

*'I **understand** perfectly the situation you are in. What would be a good solution for you?'*

Use *'understand'* to get information on the prospect's current situation.

*'Can you tell me why you are not happy with your current provider? I would like to **understand** more about your situation so that I can give you the correct solution.'*

8. STUCK

How it Works

Nobody likes to be stuck. People always want to feel that they have options. You can use the word to plant the thought in people's heads that they are not married to their current supplier and that there are other avenues they can explore.

'Stuck' is an emotive word that you use whenever you are confronted with a difficult sale or someone who's happy with their current supplier. You can even use it when they have just turned you down.

What to Say

If the prospect is using a different product or service for a long time, you can ask:

*'How long have you been **stuck** with that product? I ask because I have a great alternative for you. When is good for me to show it to you?'*

Another use is when a deal is lost and the prospect is not interested. You can always make one last attempt by saying:

*'I understand and respect your decision. I wanted to tell you about our service so that you don't feel **stuck** in the position you are today. Now you know that you don't have to be **stuck** in a situation that costs time and money. You have another option. Thank you for your time.'*

9. TO ADD TO

How it Works

'*To add to*' is one of a family of words that you can use to link what the prospect has told you about their needs to what you can offer. '*On top of, as well as*' and '*in addition to*' also belong to this family. If you don't have the exact service the prospect wants, use these words to introduce the idea of a new service or a different option.

If you know that you don't have what a prospect is looking for, think about what products and services you would like to steer your prospect towards. Then you can use these 'adding' words as a way to introduce them.

What to Say

When the prospect is finished talking, repeat what they said in your own words. This shows that you are listening. Add to what they have said by using words such as '*In addition,*' '*To add to what you have told me,*' '*On top of*' or '*as well as*' to guide the conversation in a desirable direction.

'***In addition** to X, Y and Z, our product will give you the extra lift that you need to be a step above the rest.*'

Normally, the potential client will remember what is said after these link phrases, as opposed to what is said before them. You are not disagreeing. You are simply adding to their views.

'*You might be interested to know that **as well as** the usual X, Y and Z that comes with this service, we also offer A, B and C packages as well.*'

You can also say '***To add to** what you told me, there is also this, that and the other.*'

10. QUICK

How it Works

Asking for a *'quick'* word or letting people know you will be *'quick'* conveys a sense of movement and of efficiency. You must tell people that you are not going to delay and that you understand the value of their time. When people know that you are not going to interfere with their busy day, they will relax and listen to what you have to say.

What to Say

Let the potential customer know that everything will happen fast. If you tell people you don't know how long the process will take, they will become impatient. Give them a date and timeframe where possible.

When you are cold calling or introducing yourself to a potential client, you can say:

*'Good morning, my name is Oisín. I am calling from The City Bin Co. Can I have a **quick** word?'*

I remember my dentist used to relax me by saying:

*'You will be glad to know that the process is very **quick** and easy. You won't feel a thing.'*

You are not just saying you will be *'quick'*, you are telling them that you appreciate that they have things to be doing.

11. IN THE SAME WAY THAT...YOU WILL FIND THAT...

How it Works

People buy emotionally. They make decisions based on feelings, needs, wants and emotions. When you use this phrase, you are triggering emotions and memories. You are bringing them back to a time in the past when they had a problem and that problem was resolved. Although there may be a logical process to selling and buying, if you can tap into their emotional buying power, you will be onto a winner. One way to do this is to create links and connections to these past positive emotions.

Find a positive emotional association between purchases your prospect made in the past and the purchase of your product now. The prospect will associate your product with a positive emotional experience that activates a feeling of familiarity with your product. This can be worth its weight in gold.

What to Say

Start by asking the prospect about a successful purchase that they made recently, or about a time when they changed suppliers of a service or product.

You could ask *"Have you changed any suppliers, services or products lately?"* If they answer *'Yes'* you may lead the conversation by asking, *"How did you find the change?"* and *"Did you save money and time?"*

If the feedback is positive, you can follow with *'**In the same way that** you changed suppliers to the X Company and you saved money and time, **you will find that** the positive results will be repeated when you start with our product. That would be a good feeling, wouldn't it?'*

12. DON'T THINK/ YOU ARE PROBABLY NOT INTERESTED...

How it Works

What happens when you say to somebody, *don't think about the white elephant?* They will think about the white elephant. This is a classic method, which indirectly gets your prospect to think about your product while building rapport and getting more information. When you detect a certain level of interest, you can fan the flames a little more.

What to Say

This is like showing candy to a child and saying *"You know what, you don't need it. I am going to put it back in my pocket."* Nine times out of ten, the child is going to want the candy and they will shout from the rooftops until they get it.

*'**Don't think** about this product, I want to know a little more about your system here and how it works.'*

Or you may say: *'We certainly can help you get over the line with our product, but **don't think** about our product just yet, tell me a little more about your situation.'*

Another option is to say, *'**You are probably not interested** in this, but I will give you a brief outline and I will be on my way.'*

13. YOU WILL BE SURPRISED

How it Works

Prospects don't want the hassle of changing supplier or having to learn how to use something new. One straightforward way of taking away the hassle and allowing them to relax is to take the pain out of the situation. Guide the conversation by reassuring the prospect that your product is stress free.

What to Say

'*You will be surprised how easy this will be. Now let me demonstrate why more and more of your neighbours are coming on board with this.*'

'*You will be surprised how much money you will save after switching to our product.*'

'*You will be surprised how quickly you will get in shape after only three weeks using this program.*'

'*Once you start with us, you will be surprised by the efficiency of the service and the results that will follow.*'

14. YET

How it Works

'*Yet*' allows for the possibility of growth or improvement. It is a delicate word, because you are using it to contradict what the client is saying to you, but you are showing that you respect their opinion.

You can use '*yet*' to make the presentation of a product less contrived by breaking up the descriptive adjectives that you use to boost your product's profile. When you are in a situation where you know the client isn't going to agree with you, use this word to get them on side. When you let them know that you are listening to them, they are more likely to relax and be attentive to what you have to say.

What to Say

'*You will achieve outstanding results when you use this simple **yet** remarkable product.*'

This little gem of a word is also a hot favourite when a potential client is asking about price or about the level of service before you have even started your pitch.

'*I won't talk about price just **yet**. First I will tell you about the numerous benefits you will get as an upshot of using our service.*'

You can also allay any fears your prospect may have about the level of service or standard of your product by saying:

'*We have **yet** to be matched on service. I can say this with absolute confidence, because our company is always researching better ways to deliver to our customers.*'

It is a small word, similar to '*but,*' which has a distinguishing aspect that '*but*' can't deliver.

15. DIRECTION

How it Works

Under normal circumstances, it would almost certainly not be a good idea to tell the prospect that you would like to *lead* them to a win-win situation. That will only push them away. Be direct by using direction. The word *'direction'* allows you to be direct, but in a more polite and acceptable manner. It gives you the base to show options.

You are the expert in what you sell. Be upfront and courteous. Show them all possible directions that they can take. This demonstrates your expertise in your product.

What to Say

Educate prospects about all the different options and the outcomes they have with your product.

*'Let me guide you through the different **directions** that you can take to get the top results you are looking for, while at the same time maximizing the service which we can provide for you.'*

Another great use for *'direction'* is to turn the prospect's objection around.

*'I understand Maria. I can see exactly where you are coming from, but as you know every coin has two sides. Let's turn this thing on its head and look at it from a new **direction**. Our product can save you time and money because of X, Y and Z. I believe a good **direction** for you to take would be to hold on to this for a few weeks and see the product in action with your own eyes. You will be pleasantly surprised.'*

Or you can simply say.

*'I believe a good **direction** for you would be...'*

16. SIMPLE

How it Works

When you use the word *'simple'* you will relax the potential client, because you are saying *'there are no complications'*. Your product or service is new to people and the idea of changing it may be daunting to them. They are relying on you to help them make the decision.

People will be receptive to anything that's hassle-free. Some potential clients are more averse to change than others. Using the word *'simple'* will open them up to the idea of change; help them to see it as manageable.

What to Say

*'A **simple** way to look at this is: One, you will have the benefit of X, Y and Z. Two, you will save money and time and finally, three, when you come on board with us you can be assured that you will be miles ahead of your competition.'*

This is also a great word if the prospect isn't comfortable with changing supplier.

*'The change will be so **simple** that the only way you will know that you have switched is because of the immense improvement in service.'*

*'A **simple** way to change would be to let us make a call to your current supplier on your behalf. Would you be comfortable with that?'*

Back up your use of the word *'simple'* with a clear pitch that's easy to grasp. Show the potential client that your product is simple to understand and use. If there is a lot of detail in your product, it is good to break it down and explain it with easy to remember points. At the end of your pitch, hook your prospects with a short simple summary containing three points that will drive your message home.

17. TRY

How it Works

'Try' is the key to failure. It leaves the door wide open to a lack of success. When you are trying, you are not doing. For example *'I sell'*. I don't *'try to sell.'* Delete the word *'try'* from your professional and personal vocabulary. It is not direct and it doesn't encourage the sale.

What to Say

Suggestions such as *"You should **try** to give up smoking using our new gum."* can be replaced with more solid suggestions such as *"Give up smoking today with our new gum. It is so easy."*

Don't say something to a potential client that plants the thought that the product may not work for them like *"Listen, why don't you **try** this great product and see how you get on."* Instead, you could say *"I will leave this great product with you. I have every confidence in it. You will be surprised how well this will work for you."*

Often when a deal is done, the sales person will say *"We will **try** to get that out to you tomorrow."* instead of just leaving it at *"We will get that out to you tomorrow."*

When you hear your prospect saying the word *'try'*, listen carefully, as it can imply a lack of interest and be non-committal.

18. NOW

How it Works

We all know the expression *'Where there's a will there's a way.'* When selling, you change that ever so slightly to *'Where there's a will there's a NOW.'* This is a simple phrase I came up with to use as a reminder when pitching a product or service. First you let the prospect know what it will feel like to experience the benefits from your product in the future. Then you create anticipation, enthusiasm and belief within your prospect's imagination. Finally, you must bring all those warm feelings back into the present. The best way to do this is with the use of the word *'Now'*. If your pitch is all about the future and doesn't have the magic word to bring the prospect back to the present, it can be difficult to close the sale in the moment.

What to Say

In the same way that a hypnotist will say to their clients *"You will begin to feel relaxed. Now you feel relaxed"*, you will find that *'Now'* directs the prospect's attention to the present. If you are asking the right questions in that moment, you will get the right answers.

*'You will avoid future taxes by starting **now**.'*

*'In the uncertain climate ahead, it is a smart move to put in an order **now**.'*

*'You will save your company X, Y and Z. You will be dancing on the rooftops with joy if you sign up **now**.'*

Another use for *'Now'* is to get the potential customer to say *'Now'* by asking the right closing question after your pitch summary. A little trickier but if you know the pitch is going down well it is very possible.

'You will double your saving using this product because of X, Y and Z. Now can you imagine how you will feel knowing that the job is done every time? Now imagine a stress free day with extra time on your hands because of X, Y and Z. Now feel what it might be like. Now if that could really happen for you I have one question I would like to ask you. When would be the perfect moment?'

And the magic answer you are looking for is... *'Now'*

The word *'Now'* is very powerful as a present command. It is useful when steering the conversation back on track if it has gone off the rails. Remember when you were in school and the teacher would say, *"Now turn to page 24."* We all turned to that page. If the teacher had simply said, *"turn to page 24,"* the class would probably have done it with a few daydreamers struggling on the way. When you leave out the command word, you lose control.

*'**Now** let me demonstrate three advantages of using our product.'*

The old army recruitment posters didn't just say, *"Join us"* They said *"Join us **now**."*

Put *'Now'* into your questions to command straight answers.

*'How much are you paying with your current supplier **now**?'*

*'Can you give me the business **now**?'*

*'**Now**, tell me what is not working for you with your present provider at the moment?'*

19. INSTEAD

How it Works

'Instead' is all about giving alterative options. If you give options, you give choices. Choices allow the prospect to have freedom. When prospects have the freedom to choose, they are more relaxed and will probably be more willing to buy if the want is there.

What to Say

*'**Instead** of focusing on this option, we can develop a plan that will work better with your budget. In fact, I already have a few ideas in mind.'*

*'**Instead** of doing what you are doing now you could use X, Y and Z. Even better than that, you can go with A, B and C which is something completely different.'*

'Instead' is great for getting out of a corner. If your prospect doesn't buy into your pitch *'Instead'* allows you a second chance, providing you have other options to offer.

*'Bob, I understand that this may not be for you; therefore I have something else I would like to share with you. **Instead** of going with the product I have told you about, let's look at a completely different product. After learning more about what you need, I believe this will be right up your street. Would you like to take a closer look?'*

20. COMPLIMENT

How it Works

Everybody loves to give and receive a compliment and potential clients are no different. When there is an opportunity to give one, do it. Compliments relax people and make them feel good about themselves. When they are relaxed, they will listen to what you have to say. Only pay a compliment if it comes naturally to you. If you are genuine, the prospect will pick up on that and they will return your compliment with their custom.

What to Say

Soften the ground with a compliment that's specific to your prospect.

*'I must **compliment** you on your shop layout. The space works very well.'*

*'I would like to **compliment** you on X, Y and Z.'*

If your prospect is enthusiastic about what you are presenting to them, you can praise their interest in your product. If they give you positive feedback, you can say:

*'Thank you James, your appreciation of this presentation is a great **compliment** to us.'*

A compliment is a good way to defuse a prospect's objection. Again, what you are doing here is relaxing the prospect. You are softening the objection with a compliment, which gives them kudos, while at the same time; it gives you some space to gather your thoughts.

*'James, let me **compliment** you on spotting that; in fact, that was the next thing I was going to mention to you, but you beat me to it.'*

21. EASILY/EASY

How it Works

The word *'easy'* means no effort is needed. The prospect will only move forward with you when there is no difficulty or discomfort in doing business with you. Humans are creatures of comfort and don't like change. To change suppliers or buy a new product, the potential customer must believe that it will be easy.

What to Say

When qualifying a prospect, you must ask the right questions to find out whether they are interested and what fears they have about buying. They may have a new service agreement form to sign, new people to know and there's also the fear of problems that may arise in the future not being fixed. You have to find out what fears they have about making a purchase and address them. Start by asking:

*'How **easily** could you make the change from your current supplier to us?'*

For more impact, combine *'easy'* with *'You will be surprised'* as this reinforces the impression of ease; the idea that anything is possible adds the suggestion that a change would be effortless.

*'You will be surprised at how **easy** it is to change. I believe that this will be so **easy** that the only reason that you will notice that you have a new provider is because the service will be so good.'*

22. HONOUR

How it Works

Give your word of honour and always honour your word. This simply means that you always say what you do and do what you say. A great sales person will go a step further and deliver on his promise to honour using this simple phrase, because he knows that key words like this can build trust.

Using the word '*honour*' also shows your commitment to the client, your commitment to giving them the best service they can possibly get. If you show clients that you can keep your word, you will come across as genuine and caring.

This is an old-style word, but it is as relevant today as it ever was. It tells the prospect that you respect any agreed action and that you will follow through.

What to Say

*'John, I won't just give you the run of the mill standard pitch. I will give you my word of **honour** that everything that I say I will do will be done.'*

*'John, I know this product sounds too good to be true. As night follows day I will **honour** my word and deliver all the benefits that I have been telling you about.'*

'Honour' can also be used to show gratitude for business received.

*'I am **honoured** that you have decided to hire us as your service provider.'*

Selling

Techniques, Strategies, Tips, Scripts & Inspirations

These selling techniques are signposts, pointing you in a positive direction where you can be motivated to sharpen your selling techniques. The best book on the subject maybe the one that you have yet to write. The best place to learn is where you are now, in the University of Life. Practice helps you find the best way to do what you need to do in order to deliver great sales pitches and receive the best possible outcomes.

You will learn valuable lessons that will last your whole life as a salesperson. You will have the necessary tools to educate your existing customers and potential prospects about your product. Building professional relationships using these tools will boost your confidence and product knowledge. That in turn will benefit you and convert the prospects into loyal customers.

These selling techniques, strategies, tips, scripts and inspirations have been divided into five sub-categories. Firstly, you must **create a winning mindset** *giving you the belief and determination needed when selling. Then, you will take care of your existing customers before looking for new leads by* **providing excellent customer experiences.** *You will give each prospect the opportunity to connect and engage with your* **powerful sales pitches.** *You will have* **successful sales meetings** *where you will build real relationships with the potential customer. Finally, you* **develop extraordinary selling skills** *that will give you all the tools you need to be the best you can be when selling. You will stand out from the average sales representative and sell with a new level of professionalism and confidence. Be inspired to go the extra mile to close the sale every time.*

Create a Winning Mindset

To be effective as a sales person, you must develop a strong belief in your ability to sell. You create a winning mindset by aligning your personal beliefs and attitudes with your own ability to sell and your actual selling skills. This allows you to focus on improving your selling. You accept what you know and how you perform as a sales person in this present moment. You mark out where exactly you want to be and you aim for that mark.

To create a winning mindset, think like a professional athlete. They love what they do. They do it daily. They push themselves to beat their personal best every time. They put their mind in the zone when competing for gold. They train hard and prepare for their event physically and mentally. They have weekly schedules for the training. They eat nourishing and beneficial foods. They are fit and can move fast. They know how to relax when it is time to switch off. They are okay with all outcomes. If they lose, they learn from it. If they win, they go out to better it.

Success in selling becomes achievable when you master the art of learning from your interactions with potential clients and existing customers. View the sale that goes south as an opportunity to improve personally and professionally. Know that you are not defined by your failure, but by what you do with it. When you win the sale and get the prospect over the line, look for the key factors that made the sale possible and apply them to the next potential client.

A winning mindset gives you an incentive that keeps you going all day. You are always learning. You are always hungry for more. You see the big picture as well as the small detail. You go the extra mile. You know you are a winner. Winners are confident. To be motivated to become better at selling, focus on preparation, planning, learning, and working hard towards the vision that you desire for yourself. Through this self-development, you can motivate yourself in the same way as the professional athlete and create a winning mindset. Nobody else is going to do it for you.

23. BE PREPARED FOR ALL OUTCOMES

How it Works

"Be prepared" is a Scout motto, but it isn't just for Scouts; it is for everybody, and especially for sales people. Don't just be prepared with your presentation, appearance, scripts and great tactics. Be prepared for all outcomes, in every way. Be prepared to deal with the unexpected.

When you are prepared, you will be confident. And that confidence will transfer itself to the prospect. They will be reassured by it and they will buy into it.

What to Do

The most important aspect of being prepared for all outcomes is to be okay whether you get the sale or not. This may sound strange to you. After all, you want to win the sale. You are there to win over the prospect and get the business. You have put yourself in a positive frame of mind, so you will close the sale in your favour. But if you are prepared for all outcomes, you won't be too concerned if and when you get a "no." This allows you to move on fast and go into your next meeting with a positive attitude. When you are okay with all outcomes, you will have the courage to aim higher, because the word "no" won't put you off. If you lose a sale you will go into your next meeting with your head held high. When you are okay with all outcomes, you will be able to learn from the lessons that come with every sales meeting, lost as well as won. Nothing will stop you from achieving your goals.

If a sale doesn't go your way, be prepared with an answer that will end your prospect's experience on the right note. *'That's no problem. I know our products don't suit everybody. Can you keep us in mind if the situation changes in the future?'*

Tips and Take Homes

Before you go to a meeting, check that you have all the information you need and that you have researched the prospect's company thoroughly. When you have done your homework, you will be able to answer any question. If a sale doesn't go your way, reassure yourself that you took every possible step to win the sale and that the outcome was outside of your control.

24. GET YOUR INTENTIONS RIGHT

How it Works

When I was getting married, my intention was to be in great shape for my wedding. I wanted to be fitter than I had ever been. With the guidance of a professional nutritionist, I ate very healthy and nourishing meals. I exercised three times a week under the supervision of a personal trainer. In six months, I totally transformed my body. When the day of my wedding arrived, my intention was fulfilled. I had reached my goal. However shortly afterwards, the exercise stopped and the healthy eating went out the window. I realised that I had made a fundamental error when setting this intention. My aim was to be in excellent physical condition for my wedding. It would have been a better intention to stay fit and healthy for life.

Once I had reached my intended goal, I felt as though I had crossed the finishing line. Through reflection and meditation, I became aware of my short-sighted intention. The same situation often happens in the sales process. We sign up the new customer and we make zero effort to build the relationship. Some people are in the job they are in because their last position was terrible and they needed to get out. Other people only have the ambition to pay the rent and bills. We all have good intentions. However, you need to add more detail, clarity and determination to your intentions. When your intentions are truly clear, your path in life and work will give you more fulfilment and opportunity.

What to Do

When you get your intentions right, you have more clarity and focus in the sales process and your work. To achieve this, you must know the purpose of your job and why you do it. You need to dedicate some time to reflect on what you really want to win, at work and at home. The key is to look at the big picture. Where are you now in relation to your selling success? Where do you want to be? What do you have to stop doing and what do you have to start doing to achieve this? Identifying your intentions gives you a roadmap to selling success.

Your basic intention is to close the deal and make a sale, but this isn't enough. If we only focus on getting the business, we could let ourselves down by giving a poor after service. We need to have a broader, more long-lasting intention towards the needs of the prospect.

Tips and Take Homes

Focus your intentions on closing the sale and really helping the prospect to achieve what they need and want. Put your heart into building your relationship with new customers after you close the sale, so that they become fans of you and the products you sell. They will start selling on your behalf without even knowing that they are doing it.

Also, think about your intentions towards your existing customers and the impact their happiness with your product has on your future sales. Get excited about your intentions, for yourself and towards others.

25. MOTIVATE YOURSELF

How it Works

Motivation is the driving force that helps you achieve your goals. In the case of selling, your goal is crystal clear: to convince people that your products and service have value. And if you are motivated, it makes the job a lot easier. You will be more enthusiastic and potential customers will automatically respond to this passion. A high level of motivation is one of the most important resources you can carry with you on the road to becoming the best salesperson that you can be.

Motivation isn't just about the take home pay or the everyday challenge of selling; those are just a natural part of the job. I am talking about what inspires you to go to work every single day. I am talking about belief in your own abilities, in your own integrity. You must keep your personal goals in mind, what you want for yourself and what you need to sell to achieve it.

What to Do

To get motivated, set out your goals. Visualise the success of your goals. Tap into what you believe it would feel like to be at the top of your game. When you visualise your goals, you are in a great position to achieve them.

Think about what drives you as a salesperson. Add more dynamism to your sales performance. How? You must genuinely believe in the excellence of your products and your ability to transmute that information to others. Aim to reach beyond your targets. Drive yourself by focusing on your goals. Tapping into those drivers will put you in the right frame of mind to win the sale. Let your motivation transform into enthusiasm and charm when you are with your potential customer.

Tips and Take Homes

When you motivate yourself, you motivate your customers. When you are motivated, you will find it easier to create an exciting customer experience. Fortunately, while motivation may not be a gift you are born with, it is a skill that you can acquire and sharpen every day. Use your personal and professional motivation to push out the best of your personality.

26. CREATE A VISION STATEMENT

How it Works

Just as every business has a mission statement, every sales person needs to have a personal vision statement. Vision statements are powerful because they give shape to your dreams. Your vision statement is your future story as you would like to see it. It is your vision of where you want to be, in your personal life and your work life. You can create separate vision statements for each part of your life, but it is best to start with your personal vision statement. After all, if you have ambition in your personal life, that will motivate you to succeed as a salesperson. For your sales vision statement, speak about where you see yourself and what pattern of selling you will use to get you there. That commits you to take action. You will have the confidence to start achieving excellent outcomes for you and your customers. Your customers will know that they are in the hands of a dynamic professional who can make great things happen for them.

What to Say

I am going to share my vision statement of intent for my work.

Vision statement of intent

My name is Oisín Browne and I am an excellent salesman. I am moving up the success ladder in my work. My performance is improving to heights beyond those of any of my colleagues or competitors. I am a valuable asset to my company and myself. I have succeeded and surpassed all of my targets. I have signed a publishing deal for the worldwide distribution of my book and have started my second book. I have doubled my income repeatedly, swiftly and effortlessly. I am spending quality time with my existing customers. My public speaking diary is full. I am motivating more and more people on our team to surpass their targets. I achieve all these goals and more. I am focused on reaching my targets every time.

Tips and Take Homes

Use the present tense throughout your vision statement, "I am," and "It is." and be as daring as you can. There's no need to write a novel, just a few paragraphs or bullet points. This is a personal contract of affirmations to help you reach your goal. Update your vision statement regularly. This keeps everything fresh and allows you to aim for new horizons.

27. PERSONAL AND SALES AFFIRMATIONS

How it Works

Affirmations are short positive repetitive self-talk techniques that help you to believe in yourself. They will motivate you into a more positive frame of mind, no matter what your life circumstances. When you repeat them to yourself, you reprogram your thoughts to the point where you change your beliefs. When you change your beliefs, you change your actions, because your actions are the manifestation of your beliefs. Change starts with you, the person, not the sales professional.

What to Do

Any time you have a negative thought, you can break the pattern by repeating your personal affirmations. This helps you to focus and clear your mind, putting you in a good place for the rest of the day. Through the day, repeat your selling affirmations, which will allow you to focus on your sales related goals. Here is an example of my personal affirmations and my sales related affirmations:

Personal Affirmations

- *I am physically and mentally in the best shape of my life.*
- *I am healthy and fit.*
- *I have an open heart full of joy and love.*
- *I am very comfortable in my own skin.*
- *I exercise three times a week.*
- *I eat a well-balanced and healthy diet.*
- *As a result of my actions I am healthier, wealthier and happier.*

Sales Related Affirmations

- *I am a world-class sales person.*
- *I believe in my extraordinary abilities to sell.*
- *I am always in control when I am with a prospect.*
- *My instinct guides me to lucrative opportunities.*
- *I adapt easily to new situations.*
- *I am a very confident sales person.*
- *I always close the sale easily.*

Tips and Take Homes

Write out seven personal affirmations. Repeat them every day. Any time you have a negative thought, you can break the pattern by repeating your positive affirmations. Get up each morning and automatically rhyme off your personal affirmations and focus your mind before a meeting by repeating your sales affirmations.

28. LOOK THE BUSINESS

How it Works

If you want to sell, you have got to look the part. Dress smart, look smart and sell smart. There is so much that can win or lose a sale for you before you have opened your mouth to deliver your pitch. Appearance is one of them. No matter how dynamic your delivery is, some people will rule you out if you have a stain on your jacket, or your shirt's only tucked in on one side.

When you put on your professional clothes, you will automatically go into selling mode. If you know you look good, you will feel good and that confidence will transfer itself to the prospect. For that extra burst of confidence, check yourself over before you go into a meeting, so you can straighten yourself out and tell yourself you look the business.

What to Do

Dress to impress. Choose a smart, fitted suit in neutral colours, with a clean, ironed shirt. Wear sensible, well-polished shoes. For women, put on a light coat of makeup and discreet jewellery. A lot of this is common sense, but it never hurts to be reminded of these little details.

Take a quick look in the mirror before you go into a meeting, to smooth out any last-minute glitches, like a crooked collar or rumpled hair. Buildings can be hot and we sweat more when we are nervous or excited, so check under your arms to make sure you still smell sweet. People are surprisingly interested in shoes. Always keep your shoes polished. If you have any body art, keep it carefully hidden.

Tips and Take Homes

Keep a fashion-emergency kit in your car. Use it to do some last minute grooming or to deal with any snags that may crop up. Include a change of clothes, deodorant, hand cream, a small mirror and shoe polish.

29. GET UP EARLY

How it Works

It is true that the early bird catches the worm. Getting up early is a sure-fire way to give you the best start each day. You will begin seeing the benefits immediately. You will be able to make inroads into your work before office hours start, enabling you to stay on top of your job.

When you arrive at work, you will have a head start on everybody, catching your prospect before their own day starts getting too hectic. They will be impressed by your efficiency and will appreciate the fact that you have called them at a convenient time. You will be wide-awake.

What to Do

If you normally get up at seven, start getting up at six. If you normally get up at six, start getting up at five. Give yourself time to wake up, so that you are wide awake when you do start work. You will hit the ground running, at a pace that the competitors might reach by midday.

Tips and Take Homes

When you get up early, give yourself time to relax into your day and do things you enjoy. Watch a short documentary, read a book, do something creative, go for a walk, do your exercises. If you really enjoy work and selling, plan your day or write your emails.

30. EXERCISE

How it Works

Selling is not just about how your product looks. It is about how you look and how you present yourself. When your body is fit, your mind is fit. Thirty minutes of exercise, three days a week, will keep you at the top of your game. Exercise will help you look your best. It is all about taking care of your body and your mind, to help you function in a more focused and complete way. Push yourself physically and you will see the effects mentally. You will be acting with speed and you will be thinking fast on your feet. If you are tired, overweight and without energy, it will be harder to sell your merchandise. Your movements are slower. You give up easier. If you want to sell, you need energy. Exercise will give you the extra energy to put passion into your pitch. You will automatically see a difference in your selling and motivation levels. The benefits of exercise will far outweigh the inconvenience. You will not only have more energy for selling, you will have more energy within yourself and this will boost your overall confidence and health. When we are in shape, we have higher levels of energy, and a more positive outlook. Prospects will be drawn to this positive outlook. Ultimately, taking exercise makes it easier to sell. A better body means better business.

What to Do

The simple things you can do at home can be the best. Go for a walk or a run. A few push-ups or sit-ups can help too. If you don't know where to start, you can always ask. You don't need to throw yourself into professional sports, or spend hours in a gym. It is easy to fit a walk or a short workout into your day. Exercise goes hand in hand with diet. Giving yourself an exercise routine and a balanced diet is like checking your car for oil and water.

Tips and Take Homes

Find a way to incorporate exercise into your routine. Join a gym that offers 30 and 60-minute circuit training programmes. For a little motivation, team up with your colleagues and work together to keep in shape. Back up your new exercise regime by drinking lots of water and eating healthy food. Cut back on the treats and sweets. Include plenty of fruit and vegetables in your daily food intake. Speak to a personal trainer and nutritionist to get expert advice and work out a personal plan that will suit your busy selling diary.

31. BELIEVE IN YOUSELF

How it Works

When I approached the editor of the local newspaper looking to write a weekly column in the business section, I didn't doubt that I could write the column and I didn't doubt that he would say yes. On the morning that I met Declan Varley, the editor of *The Galway Advertiser*, I pitched my idea to him. Although I had a lot of experience of writing press releases and business proposals within the music and waste industries, I never studied journalism or had any experience writing for traditional media.

I believed in my idea so much that the energy and enthusiasm was captured in every word that I uttered to Declan during my five-minute meeting. I followed up the meeting with examples of my writings. Within one month, I had my own bi monthly column called 'Drop the Monkey Business' on the front page of the business section of this local newspaper. I believed in myself and through the conviction of this belief, I created a power that allowed the editor to believe in me with the same confidence and conviction.

What to Do

To believe in yourself is to have an "I can do it" attitude about your capabilities in life. Know and believe that you have the power you need to succeed in all that you set out to do. Acknowledge yourself as an achiever. Fulfil your potential by building your belief in yourself. You will achieve more. You will get opportunities that you didn't see before. You will stand by all your decisions finding it easier to deal with difficulties. Set out new goals in new areas even if they seemed impossible in the past. Empower yourself to accomplish anything you set out to do. This will cause you to lose all fear and grow your confidence.

Tips and Take Homes

Before you set your eyes on a new goal, remind yourself that you are capable of achieving whatever you set out to achieve, for you and for others. When in meetings, your confidence will come across when you are talking to your prospects and people will buy into that confidence. Believe in yourself and in your abilities. Believe in your product. Believe in your prospects. Believe in the end result. Feed your belief with passion by setting new goals for your life and for work.

32. BE YOURSELF TO SELL YOURSELF

How it Works

It not the product that sells, it's the person behind the product. People buy from people. If the potential customer feels they can relate to you on a human level, they will trust you more. Business comes a lot easier when you have built trust on a personal level.

What to Do

When you are with a prospect, just be yourself. Show them the interesting side of you, the human being who has a life outside work. Talk about your hobbies. Tell them about your family and kids. Everyone can relate to those kinds of topics and it helps to get the conversation started.

When you speak to people on a personal level, you can connect with them on a personal level. This opens up the possibility of leaving a positive first impression. The sale process is important, but if you don't add that little bit of you into the mix, you risk not making a very significant connection with your prospect.

Tips and Take Homes

The pitch is important, but the magic ingredient is you. It is you that the prospect will remember. Find a common ground with the prospect. It will be easier for you to share your passion and to be authentic.

33. LEARN TO LET GO

How it Works

Sometimes emotions can get the better of us, after a bad day or a deal that didn't close. When you walk away from a meeting frustrated because the conversation didn't go well, your frustration will spill over into your next meeting and affect the outcome.

But when you accept all outcomes, you let go of negative emotions and keep your head clear. You won't be bringing any baggage to the next prospect's table. Letting go is not a sign of weakness. It puts you in control.

When you let go, any nerves will fall away, because you won't fear a negative outcome. You will speak and act with conviction and potential customers will pick up on the vibes of confidence you give off. It is like dating. People will steer clear if you sound desperate. Let go of that fear and you will turn your fortunes around.

What to Do

After a frustrating meeting, take three deep breaths and feel the emotion leave you. Accept the outcome and remember that this is no reflection on your abilities as a salesperson. If you find it hard to let go, schedule some time in your week, a half hour brainstorm on your own or with a colleague, where you can examine the results of particular meetings.

Tips and Take Homes

Don't organise meetings back to back. Allow for timeouts to deal with any frustration or disappointment. Go for a coffee, ring a friend or read a newspaper. Do some breathing exercises. They are brilliant for relaxation and letting go of any tension.

34. EXPAND THE SALES TEAM

How it Works

The sales department consists of every customer you deal with, past, present and future. It is the customers you have won and plan to win. Your sales department is every staff member you have and ever had. As well as being a sales person, you are the motivator for all of these people. You need to let all your work colleagues know exactly what you do in your day-to-day job. Explain to them your definition of an ideal lead or perfect fit for the services you offer.

What to Do

You need to get everybody on board. No matter what the job title is for the people working in your company, they all have a duty to sell. Sell yourself to the people you work with before you go out selling your products to potential customers. This is a great way to obtain referrals and catch any potential leads that may slip through the net.

Tips and Take Homes

Send everybody in your company a profile of the typical prospect that you are looking out for and show gratitude to those who take a moment from their job to send you a lead, or even help you get the prospect over the line. Remember, all these guys have their own work to get on with, so just ask them to be an extra pair of eyes and ears when it comes to potential sales.

35. RELAX

How it Works

The best way to relax is to empty your mind of all thoughts, much like cleaning a whiteboard and leaving it blank for a while. Being relaxed is crucial to success in sales. It gives you confidence and when you are confident, you will overcome all obstacles. If you are relaxed, it is impossible to be nervous and your calm demeanour will reassure your potential customers.

When you are relaxed, it is easier to move on with good grace when there appears to be no fit between your product and your prospect's needs. You won't be desperate for a sale and you will keep the relationship with the prospect intact.

What to Do

Relaxation exercises are easy to do. First, find a quiet place to sit. Switch off all devices that might distract you, like mobile phones and radios. Make yourself comfortable and relax into your seat. Close your eyes. Now it is time to start clearing your mind and relaxing your body. Start by concentrating on your breathing. Count to four as you breathe in through your nose. Hold for two and count to four again as you exhale. Then hold for two with an empty diaphragm and repeat for 5-10 minutes. You can add in some affirmations or positive visualisations as you breathe.

Tips and Take Homes

Train yourself to breathe before, during and after a pitch. If a prospect is coming up with objection after objection, take a breath, smile, relax and reply to the objections. If you are relaxed, your potential client will be relaxed and will be open to suggestions.

36. FIND THE FUN FACTOR

How it Works

Having fun is one of the most important laws of selling. After all, if you are not enjoying the experience, how can you expect to give your best? Have fun with your customers by making them laugh. When you are having fun, you are passionate about your work and that passion is contagious. The prospect will want more of this fun vibe.

There is a time and place for everything and if you are nervous, you may misjudge the humour, especially with a client who just wants to get down to business. It is important not to take yourself too seriously, After all, it is only a job and we are all human.

What to Do

Don't worry if you are not a comedian. It is more important to be natural and show that you enjoy the lighter side of life. Injecting a bit of humour will also make your sales pitches stand out. People will remember the one who made them laugh. Use humour to show that you are comfortable in your own skin. Humour is highly individual, but a little light banter, such as friendly teasing about rival sports teams, will always break the ice. Resist the urge to act the clown. Always keep it professional. Enjoy the fun of winning and even the fun of losing.

Tips and Take Homes

Humour also works well in the office. If you get uptight before meeting prospects, do some role-playing with your colleagues. This has very real benefits, because it will help you to isolate and tackle problems you may not have realised were there. You will also be able to let off some steam and that light mood will give you confidence at meetings.

37. BOOST YOUR COMMISSION

How it Works

A lot of companies build their sales model on commission. Commission is a payment paid in addition to your salary and sometimes instead of a salary, to motivate you to reach and exceed monthly targets. Normally, it is based on the value of sales achieved. Wanting a bigger commission doesn't mean you are greedy. It means you will be closer to achieving your dreams. The most important thing is how you view commission. If money is not a big driver for you, let it be an incentive for you to buy the things you want and deserve. Many things motivate us and most people will say that their jobs aren't all about the money. But ultimately, we are in it to win it.

What to Do

Aim for the dream car you always wanted, a holiday or a new gadget that is out on the market. Find pictures that relate to your goal, a tropical beach to represent a holiday, a dollar sign for savings or a car you would love to drive and put them where you can see them, in your diary, on your fridge door, and in your office. Use the images as a tool to motivate you to boost your commission. There is nothing more powerful then visualising your end result. The commission is the carriage that will take you there.

Tips and Take Homes

Write a list of the ways that your life would improve if you earned more commission. Set your goals and go after them. Your commission will only rise when you close more sales. When you prove your ability to hit your targets and beyond, you put yourself in a position to renegotiate your commission.

38. INTRODUCE A SWITCHING OFF RITUAL

How it Works

I am one of the lucky guys. Between my office and my home, which are five minutes apart on foot, there is a hotel with a beautiful little coffee shop and a gym. In the morning before going to the office I start at the hotel, where I take ten minutes to enjoy a warm cup of green tea. When I finish my work, I go to the gym for 20 minutes. Sometimes I will do a full on work out and other times I enjoy the pool and the steam room facilities. This is my switching off ritual. It works the same way as a light switch you turn on and off. Once I have my green tea each morning, I am switched on and ready to go. When I walk out of the gym each evening, I am really switched off from my work and ready to embrace my family and home life. No matter how much you enjoy selling, when the job is done, switch off. A good motto to apply to your work-life balance is: *'Work to live, don't live to work'.* Tomorrow is another day. Being able to switch off will help you recharge your batteries and keep you fresh.

What to Do

Introduce a switching off ritual into your routine. This will help you to form new habits that celebrate the change from work to home. For example, read a page or a chapter of a novel when you arrive home. Go to the gym and work out. If you wear a suit for work, change out of it and into something more casual and comfortable when you arrive home. Have a bath or a shower to wash all the worries of work away. This will help you to enter your home life fresh and alert.

Tips and Take Homes

Different strategies work for different people. Make plans to do things that you can look forward to outside of your working hours. To really unplug, you should switch off your phone, laptop or any other devices related to your work. You need to draw a line in the sand that clearly shows work on one side and rest and play on the other side. Make a rule to never speak about work outside work.

39. LOVE WHAT YOU DO

How it Works

You can waste many hours of the day thinking about some aspect of work that you don't like or you can redirect the same energy to a positive outlook by just doing it. With the latter, you get the task done faster, with more focus and the probability of a favourable outcome. Becoming brilliant at selling happens when you do more than just understand the products you sell and the small interactions that allow you to connect with your prospects and customers. You have to love what you do. You may not do what you love, but you certainly can love what you do. This is not a 'fake it until you make it solution'. This is about tapping into the source of what makes you feel good in the day and expanding that feeling. When you are satisfied about your job and enjoy the process, you will sell more. Starting with the small things will make it easier to do business.

I have spent years selling bin bags and skips, which are not the trendiest product to sell. In the beginning, I didn't enjoy the selling process, not because of the product or people. I was frustrated with the fact that I was always in traffic jams going from one meeting to another. It took over my thought process, to the point where I realised it was affecting my life. When greeting a prospect *"the terrible traffic"* was the first thing I would mention. Going *"back into that traffic"* was the first thing I would think about when leaving a prospect's place of business. I changed this way of thinking by focusing on the things I loved within my working day, such as talking to customers and prospects, tea breaks and listening to the radio. From that moment on, traffic jams never bothered me as I got so much enjoyment from the radio talk shows while driving from one client to another. Once I replaced the habit of negative thinking about the traffic jam, it affected my sales for the better. I was happier, more relaxed and I was more focused on my tasks. The prospects picked up on this. It balanced my working day so much that now when I am in a traffic jam I don't even notice.

What to Do

Strengthen your position by changing how you view the overwhelming or disheartening tasks in your diary. Find the little gems within your working day where you are comfortable, forget about the actual job and focus on the positive moments.

Seek out the simple, non-work related things that happen and tap into them. Take the time to enjoy your breakfast, lunch and dinner. Listen to the radio while driving between meetings. Have interesting conversations with every interaction. Seek them out and build on them, right up to the big prize of winning the sale.

Tips and Take Homes

Acknowledge and accept where you currently are in your career cycle in order to find the happiness within your professional life. If you are thinking that you are in a bum job, selling a bum product or doing some bum task, you are going to trip yourself up before you even get to the starting line. Radiate enthusiasm from the enjoyment of doing the small things. Make the small jobs the reason to start the day and win the sale. This allows you to have a clear and positive frame of mind when talking to prospects. This means you and the person with whom you are talking will be relaxed, creating a preferred atmosphere for the sale to materialise.

40. GET BACK ON YOUR BIKE!

How it Works

If you lose a sale, get back on your bike and sell. It is that simple. The more you analyse, the more you will start to fear the worst-case scenario, which won't help you win your next sale. Think back to when you were a child, riding your bike for the first time. You didn't do a risk assessment or stress test before getting up and going as fast as you could. You didn't think *'what if I fail to reach my desired speed?'* or *'what if I fall?'* You didn't put the bike away after you fell. When you did fall, your parent's response was to tell you it was nothing to worry about and to get back on your bike, which is what you did. You had no fear of failure; you didn't care what other people were thinking. It was all about being free, enjoying the moment, and inducing a self-fulfilling happiness of just being, doing and succeeding.

What to Do

Learn to enjoy the process of selling rather than worrying about what might go wrong or trying to do it perfectly. You can never 100% predict or determine the exact outcome of your interactions with prospects. Reduce your fear of failure by doing rather than thinking and talking. Make a commitment to view failures as experiences. Think as you did when you were a child riding a bike for the first time. Be fearless. Have a great sense of self-belief and determination.

Tips and Take Homes

Get yourself a bike and ride it! Or sell it! The achieving is in the action and the enjoyment of the action, not necessarily in the result. Don't look on losing the sale as a failure. See it as another step in improving your skill. Embrace the risk and above all enjoy it. The outcome can't always be the most important thing on your mind. Know that you will get there in the end. Just go for it!

Providing Excellent Customer Experiences

Existing customers and potential prospects want much more than a purchase. They want an experience. The experience is what happens before, during and after the actual purchasing of the product. Customers buy into the experience as well as the purchase. You have a responsibility to give an experience that makes people talk about your product in a positive light and leaves them wanting to come back for more.

To master the mechanics of true selling, you must understand the importance of building and maintaining customer relationships. To leave a great first impression with potential prospects, you must look after your existing customers. When you have a genuine desire to give your existing customers a delightful experience, they will reward you with their "Wow" stories. Bringing these "Wow" stories to a potential client adds substance to your pitch.

Telling a prospect about somebody else's experience with your product is more beneficial than talking directly about what you sell or how something works. To find these "Wow" stories, you have to connect with your clients on a meaningful level. You have to care.

You need to connect and reconnect with your customers. Call in on your customers continuously and talk to them about their level of satisfaction, their experience and feedback on your product. Call them before they call you. It is better to be proactive as opposed to reactive. You need to touch base with all customers that come on board, without exception. Be friendly. Remember the names of your customers. Show respect. Listen to the customer, answer their questions and learn from them. Say thank you. Be responsive and offer real solutions in real time. Consider the value of their experience with you and your product in future sales. The potential customer wants to know what other people who bought your product thought of it. Your job is to point them to this information.

As a sales person who gives great customer service and after-care, you must understand that these excellent customer experiences create loyalty. Loyalty creates fans. Fans follow you. They buy more from you. They become champions of you and what you sell.

41. LOOK AFTER YOUR EXISTING CUSTOMERS

How it Works

When you are chasing after new customers, it can be easy to let your existing customers slip through the cracks, especially if they don't buy from you frequently. If you don't look after your existing customers, somebody else will. You must go beyond the call of duty and really care for your clients, their businesses and what is happening in their world. Don't just meet customers, connect with them by becoming an expert in providing excellent customer service and exceeding all their expectations. Treat all customers as the valuable asset that they are. The customers that you retain and satisfy automatically become a vital part of your sales team. By looking after your existing customers you will become more educated in what you sell, understanding your product from the buyer's perspective.

What to Do

Get to know your customers. Mark bi-monthly calls to your regular clients in your calendar and call them. Get feedback from your clients on your service, products and people. Ask them if they are happy with the service they are getting and if there is anything that you can do to improve their experience with the product. Get them talking about you and your product. Get them selling on your behalf. Ask them what is new in their work. They will appreciate the fact that you have remembered them and they will give you information that will be extremely useful. Ask them if there is anything else you can do for them.

Tips and Take Homes

Take every opportunity to build relationships with your clients. If it is a client's birthday, send them a note wishing them a great day. If a customer has a baby, send flowers. Check that all their details are up to date. By engaging with the customers on a human level, you build relationships that last.

42. TREAT YOUR CUSTOMERS WITH RESPECT

How it Works

In the rush to land the sale, never lose sight of the fact that prospects and customers are people first and foremost. Whatever happens, you must treat them with respect at all times. When you show respect, customers will feel valued for their choices.

Customers and prospects have the right to decide whether to buy your product or not without being pressurised. They have a right to privacy. When you visit them, respect their place of work and respect their place of residency. Respect your prospects as people, because they are people. Do not speak to a prospect in any negative way.

What to Say

Respect the customer's right and the prospect's right to engage or not engage with you, your company or product. Be polite and understanding. If your product is not for them, show your respect by saying:

'I totally understand that this product isn't a good fit for you. I accept and respect your decision. Thank you kindly for your time'

Tips and Take Homes

Understand that while you are selling to prospects and communicating with clients, you represent yourself, your company and your product and any lack of respect towards others will not be good for business. This doesn't mean that you have to put up with any lack of respect yourself. Treat others, as you would expect others to treat you. If a prospect is not respectful towards you, thank them for their time and walk away.

43. BE YOUR OWN BEST CUSTOMER

How it Works

Using your own product helps you to understand and explain the values and benefits of it in a more convincing light. If you want to sell convincingly, you need to put your money where your mouth is and sample your own products. When you know your product inside out, your enthusiasm for your product will be a lot more genuine. You will be more relaxed in delivering your pitch and the prospect will see that you understand your prospect from a user's perspective.

What to Do

Demonstrate that you have used the product successfully. This shows that you have walked the walk and increases the customer's confidence in your product. Know your own product inside out. Use it. Test it. Learn its strengths and its weaknesses. A prospect will appreciate it when you say:

'The one small thing that bothered me when I signed up to this product at the start was this, but here is how I got over that. I have been flying ever since. I can vouch for the fact that it works perfectly because I use it myself.'

Tips and Take Homes

When you are road testing your products, always look at them from the potential customer's point of view. As well as asking yourself what you like about the product, be sure to give yourself a devil's advocate opinion of the product. This way you will be able to pinpoint all the possible issues that may arise with the use of your product. You can then seek customer-focused solutions based on your own experience. With confidence, you will be able to answer any future questions that prospects or clients put to you.

44. EMPATHISE WITH YOUR CUSTOMERS

How it Works

Empathy in selling and customer service is all about your ability to place yourself in your client's shoes. When you empathise, you turn from a salesperson into a friend. You are showing people that their feelings and opinions matter. Everyone loves to be heard and understood, especially when they are focusing on a problem.

Empathy is a key factor when doing business, because when you can see your product from the view of your prospect, you will anticipate potential problems long before they surface. Empathy is when you know the gains for both the client and yourself.

What to Say

Use empathy to emphasise the sale from the perspective of the prospect or client and not you or your company. Empathy is a powerful tool in sales and customer service. It is being able to say:

'I understand completely, and if I was where you are right now, I would be asking the very same questions.'

'I was once in the place where you are now. Do you know what got me through?'

Tips and Take Homes

Set your own views completely to the side, even if you don't agree with the customer. You are there to do a job, to represent the company, not to voice your own opinions or share your own woes. When you are empathising with your customer or a prospect, they will tell you what they need and you can then demonstrate how you can help or how your product will solve their problem. This will tell them that they are buying from you, rather than you selling to them.

45. SHOW YOUR GRATITUDE

How it Works

The words "thank you" really matter to people. People like to feel appreciated, to feel that what they do has a positive impact on others. As a salesperson, you are asking for a considerable commitment from people, to give up their time, to sign on the dotted line or to part with hard earned cash. When you say "thank you," you acknowledge that commitment. You are showing that the sales process doesn't just flow one way.

What to Say

A simple *"thank you"* can be a very powerful tool when looking to move the process to a close.

- *Thank you for your time.*
- *Thank you for listening.*

Even when things are not going your way, a *"thank you"* can take the stress out of the situation and put everyone at ease.

- *Thank you for sharing.*
- *Thank you for pointing that out to me.*

When the sale closes in the right direction:

'I am very grateful to you for coming on board with this product.'

Gratitude is even more important when the sale doesn't go to plan; it helps you end your conversation on the right note.

'I want to thank you for your frankness, your time and for making a decision today.'

Tips and Take Homes

Your customers have brought you to where you are today. If you have customers who are extremely loyal, sending a hand written thank you card will show them that you are willing to go the extra mile for that loyalty.

46. GIVE GIFTS TO YOUR CUSTOMERS

How it Works

Giving gifts has many benefits. It is the ultimate way to show your appreciation to your customers. It can be a light-hearted conversational starting point before getting down to business in the meeting.

What to Do

A small gift to a prospect or a customer helps to create trust and build rapport. Give a pen, a book or even an email with a positive motivational message that relates to a conversation you had. Print out an essay related to your product or the topic on the table for discussion and give it to everybody attending the meeting. You could introduce it by saying:

'I have brought you all a little gift, just to show my appreciation of your continuing loyalty to our service.'

Tips and Take Homes

Give gifts to celebrate different events in your customer's timeline with you. Send them a personal note on their birthday wishing them a great day. When you start a relationship with a new customer, send a welcome pack. Celebrate their first, third or fifth year anniversary as a loyal customer and get the champagne out if they have been buying from you for 10 years.

Always tell the customer that you are going to give or send them something before you do. It builds trust, because if you promise a gift and then give it, it shows them that you will deliver. It puts in place a pattern that can be followed, that you promise and you deliver.

47. BE A BUSINESS COACH

How it Works

Interact with your customer by being a business coach to them. Offer some ideas or suggestions that can help them achieve their goals. Coaching means educating the customer with experiences you have had and that they can apply to their business or life. Share what you know from the techniques you use, right through to your success stories and the lessons that you have learned. People don't like to feel they are just being sold to; they want to engage with you and learn from you. They want to know why and how things work for you and how they too can make it work for them. Show them.

What to Do

Ask them what they do and what their goals are. Put forward an idea or maybe a contact with a similar interest. If you don't know about the theme at hand, stick to what you know. Tell them how they could possibly approach their business or interest from a sales point of view. Compliment them and offer your free professional insight. Be willing to share your experience with customers.

Tips and Take Homes

You can create a bond with your customer by offering valuable advice. The customer will see you as an expert, someone who knows what they are doing. When you give advice, you give of yourself. You are generous with your time and your knowledge. People will remember and associate these nuggets of advice with you.

48. UPDATE YOUR CUSTOMERS

How it Works

People love to know that they are on the inside track. Giving new information on what is hot and what is not in your industry is a good way to connect with customers. Update them on new offers, changes in your service, or the progress of new products. This guarantees their loyalty.

By circulating information frequently, you reinforce your name and product, leading to product awareness and a sense of familiarity. Customers will become familiar with your product and people trust what is familiar. Remember that old proverb "out of sight, out of mind." If you keep people up to date, they won't forget you.

What to Do

Update your prospects and existing customers regularly. Let them know about new products or your latest blog. Keep regular contact with each individual customer by phone and email. Keep it short, sweet and to the point:

'Hi John. Just ringing to keep you in the loop about some new products we are developing. We want to give our regular clients a chance to avail of a discount before we release them on the market.'

Tips and Take Homes

Aim to give weekly, fortnightly and monthly updates to your prospects and existing customers. Adding competitions to your updates will encourage them to buy in. Start a blog about the product you sell. This is a useful tool that you can direct customers to when you have something you to share with them.

49. BUY FROM YOUR CUSTOMERS

How it Works

It is good practice to buy from people that buy from you; it reinforces the fact that you are doing business together. This secures and builds the relationship while placing an emotional value on the transaction and the people involved. In other words, your existing clients will be less likely to jump ship and sign up with the competition.

What to Do

Don't be afraid to put the sellers to the test when you are buying, while still being polite. Whether you are buying something small and simple, such as a cup of tea, or something big like a kitchen for a house, throw up some objections to see how others answer you. Question the price, the quality or the size of the product. Ask for a discount. Say that you know somebody in another company who can get you a deal. Tell them you can get one 20% cheaper on the other side of town. Ask them can they throw in something extra. Rehash objections that you yourself have received in the past. This is a great way to learn.

Tips and Take Homes

Always be courteous, in the knowledge that you sell and represent your company and its products. Being an objective buyer is a great way to learn about the buying experience from the prospect's perspective. You will learn more about how your customers operate, what they value and what they need from you.

50. RESELL TO YOUR CUSTOMERS

How it Works

When you are updating an existing product or launching a new product, use the opportunity to resell to your existing customers. Although your primary focus should be to chase new business, don't forget about the customers that have used your products and services to date. If they are using your products that means you can sell to them again when your company introduces upgrades, or a brand-new line of products. They offer an ideal sales opportunity – you are preaching to the converted. You will be surprised at how much extra selling can be done by communicating with old and existing customers. You can create opportunities to resell, up sell and upgrade.

What to Do

This is all about regular communication with your clients. When your company upgrades its existing products, or introduces new ones, take the time to tell your existing customers about it. Phone them, write to them, and advertise on the invoices that you send to them. Benefit from a stronger relationship by keeping them updated regularly.

Tips and Take Homes

When you have reconnected with all your existing clients, use the same techniques as an opportunity to connect with new leads. You will have all your possible objections ironed out and your pitch will be tighter due to the consistent conversations with your own customers. Let them know that you have contacted all of your own clients with the good news of a new product and that you wouldn't like them to miss out.

51. INVITE YOUR CUSTOMERS FOR COFFEE

How it Works

Invite customers out for a coffee or a quick lunch meeting. It brings your relationship into a neutral and relaxed environment. You will have a chance to get to know each other in an informal setting and to relate to each other on a human level. It is also a way of rewarding them for their loyalty to your company.

What to Do

During your coffee meeting, get a feel for what sort of person the customer is, what their tastes are, what drives them. You can then put that knowledge to good use when you are back in the sales environment. Outside the office the customer is relaxed, they are more open to listening to ideas and suggestions.

Tips and Take Homes

If you have a large customer base it may not be possible to meet every one of them. Organise a coffee morning in a local coffee house and invite all your customers to come. As well as thanking your customers for their loyalty you will be giving them an opportunity to network.

52. RECONNECT WITH CUSTOMERS

How it Works

It is very important to look after your existing customers before you go after the competition's customers. You have to reconnect regularly. Tap into your own source of opportunity with your existing customers. Aim to reconnect once or twice a year. It will give you a chance to clear up any doubts they may have about your product, increase your orders, confirm that you have the correct details, build rapport and get referrals.

What to Say

The script is broken up into four parts. Firstly, greet them, wish them well and confirm all the details such as emails, address and phone numbers. Secondly, ask if they are happy with the service. This is a great chance for you to deal with any problems they may have before they come to you three months down the line with a bigger problem. The job here is to put any issues that they may have with your product or company to bed. Thirdly, let them know about your special offers. Ask them if they would like to make another order. Finally, at the closing of the call, thank them for their business and wish them well.

'Hi Mary, this is Oisin from The City Bin Co., Mary, this is just a quick call to wish you a happy new year. Mary, I am updating my database and I want to make sure I have all your correct details.'

'Are you happy with the service that you are currently receiving from us?'

'Mary, before I let you go, our annual special price week has started today. You can save X, Y and Z. Will I put you down for an order?'

'Mary, I want to thank you for your continued business. I look forward to seeing you at the end of the week. Have a great day.'

Tips and Take Homes

You don't need to see these clients face to face or spend hours with a small few. A quick phone call can do the job. Always keep the conversion short and sweet. If there is no answer, leave a message and make a note to call back at a later date. A great time to reconnect with customers is January. You can wish them a happy New Year.

Effective Sales Pitches

To develop and deliver an effective sales pitch, you need to turn your product presentation into a valuable conversation. You are looking to interact with the prospect, build a relationship, and tap into their emotional buying power. You need to build rapport, ask the right questions, listen to the prospect attentively, and offer them a valued solution to their problem. You need to be able to answer their doubts and queries about you, your company and your product.

Your intention needs to be focused on having engaging dialogue, using simple, clear and direct language that the prospect can understand. Together, you must go though the nuts and bolts of what you are selling. A successful pitch isn't about selling or buying. It is a two-way conversation with a conclusion that amounts to an agreed transaction that benefits all parties.

The product that you sell is a solution to a prospect's problem. While you must prepare in advance, keep in mind that no one pitch fits all. Prospects are people and all people are unique and individual in their buying process. They buy on price, quality, needs, and wants. While some follow the crowd, others buy on the basic feelings of *'Well, I just had a nice conversation with a nice person that listened to me and understood me.'*

Engage in interesting conversation with the prospect to show them that you are passionate about helping them and passionate about your product. Use action verbs and metaphors to trigger their imagination. Guide the conversation by relating to the way that they speak. Ask questions, listen and offer solutions. Demonstrate the value and benefits of what you sell. Ask for the business.

53. ELEVATE YOURSELF WITH AN ELEVATOR PITCH

How it Works

One of the most important things you should know is how to introduce yourself and your product to others. I am talking about your elevator pitch, something you can say quickly which simply defines you and your product. You should always have a short summary you can use at a moment's notice to introduce yourself. Attention spans are getting shorter and time is at a premium. You need to be able to get your message across quickly. Your elevator pitch will promptly clarify who you are, what you offer and how you can be of service.

What to Say

Prepare a few different introductions that you can deliver from memory. Keep it easy to chop and change in the moment, depending on where you are and who you are with. This will allow you to adapt to different situations and different audiences.

Write it, learn it, rehearse it and deliver it with great confidence. Nobody knows what you are selling like you do. Here is an example of an elevator pitch I give when I am introducing myself, my company and our products to potential clients at business networking groups.

'Good morning, my name is Oisín Browne. I work in customer service with The City Bin Co. We are an award winning waste and recycling company, with our headquarters located in Oranmore. We service Dublin City and Galway City. That's East to West and the stops in-between. We work with domestic, commercial and industrial markets. That's everything from your household, your hotel to your hospital. The City Bin Co. has a drop off centre where the public can bring materials. The City Bin Co. recently entered the home heating oil market. We now offer this service to all households in Galway city. Like us on our social media pages to be in with a chance to win our monthly competitions. Thank you".

Preparation is the key to an excellent elevator pitch. Writing your pitch will help you remember what you want to say and deliver it with confidence.

As with all presentations, your pitch needs to be memorable, so keep it short and direct. When you are delivering your pitch, use a maximum of three points at a time and then move on so it is easier to remember. For example: *"We work with 1) Domestic 2) Commercial and 3) Industrial markets."*

Tips and Take Homes

Perform your pitch to every audience possible. It will give you the opportunity to get new prospects and to fine-tune your quick fire introduction of your product giving you a smooth delivery. Even the most experienced among us will feel a little nervous from time to time. Remember to relax; people want to hear what you have to say. Nobody will notice if you have made a slip-up.

Practice is the ingredient that helps a professional singer hit the notes every time. Practice does not always make perfect, but it does make it personal and a personal pitch is priceless.

54. THE SECRET LANGUAGE OF SELLING

How it Works

Positive body language and appropriate verbal communication are vital tools when you are selling your product to the potential client. Delivering a pitch isn't just about what you say; it is about how you say it; your words and your body language. We process a huge amount of information from non-verbal cues. First impressions do last; therefore, your non-verbal communication is very important. Your posture, your personal traits, your general conduct, your gestures and your physical appearance can have a huge impact on the success of your sales. How you smile, how you laugh, your eye contact and even your handshake will show a prospect how confident you are about your product and about how well it will work for them.

What to Do

To gain the most out of your verbal communication, speak with your own voice and accent, in other words, be yourself. Pronounce you words clearly. Deliver your pitch in a relaxed, confident tone. The prospect will pick up on that. If you speak too fast, the prospect may feel rushed or may not understand you. Take a few breaths between points to stop yourself from rushing through your pitch. Allow your language to flow in a non-aggressive manner. Listen to the words that your prospect uses and mirror the way that they speak. As a sales person, you will be very persuasive if you speak the prospect's language. You will be subconsciously sending the message that you are tuned into them and they will feel a connection with you as a result.

You can pick up clues to how your prospect thinks by listening to the words that they use and the way that they speak. People experience the world in three ways: auditory, kinaesthetic, and visual. An auditory based prospect may say *"That sounds good"*. Or *"I hear what you are saying"*. A kinaesthetic based prospect will use words related to the muscle senses such as to touch, to feel, or to grab. *"That doesn't really grab my attention"*. Or *"That sure does feel good to me"*. A Visual based prospect may say *"I see what you are saying"*. Or *"I am not sure if this is what I am looking for."* By speaking their language, you can connect with them in a way that they will recognise and relate to on a subconscious level.

Tips and Take Homes

Always greet prospects with a smile and a firm handshake. Echo their style of speech so that they will relate to what you are saying at a subconscious level, which will help you create a powerful connection. Don't use obscene or offensive words. When you are talking to prospect, don't look at your mobile, stare at the ground, or start looking around to see who might be beside you.

Be aware of how you move, how you use your body and how you speak. It will be easier for you to stamp out body language that may make a prospect nervous. Don't cross your arms or legs. Keep good eye contact by looking in the direction of the prospect. This lets them know you are concentrating solely on them.

55. TEN COMMON OBJECTIONS WITH RESPONSES

How it Works

An objection is a valid excuse in the mind of the prospect for not buying. When you overcome an objection you keep the sales process moving towards the sale being closed. End your answers with a guide question that will let the prospect tell you about your product's good points, or qualify the next stage of the sale. Getting an objection doesn't always mean *"No."* It can mean, *"Give me more information."*

What to Say

1. **The other guys are cheaper. They beat you hands down on price.** Before I continue, let me ask you a question. If you had a choice between a brand new BMW and a beat-up second hand car, which would you choose? Let's be honest. If our product was as cheap as theirs, we would be telling you that our product is only as good as their product and only has the same value as theirs. We both know that's not true. You will be getting a better product for your money. What are the benefits of our product that most interest you?

2. **I had a bad experience using your product and will never go there again.** I understand completely. Tell me what happened? I can tell you with the utmost honesty that our company has taken giant leaps over the past year to improve the quality of the product and to make sure those kinds of mishaps don't repeat themselves. This reminds me of a time two years ago when I was camping in the north of Spain. I was very disappointed with the service and quality of the campsite. I told my wife that I would never return. She convinced me to return the following year and I was amazed to find it was a changed place. The workers at the campsite had received training in the meantime. They were now polite and professional. The quality improved so dramatically that the campsite won a 'best campsite in Europe' award. I couldn't believe it. I was so impressed and glad that we returned. You will find that we have done the same with our product and our team. Let's turn that bad experience into a great experience. You will be surprised at the results. Would you give it a go?

3. **You guys are the big guns in town. I want to support the local guys.** That's not the first time I have heard that. It is such a lovely compliment. Thank you. I can see how you would think that. In reality, the company I work for was founded by and run by two locals. They are so professional and pay such close attention to every detail that a lot of local people have started to buy from them. Actually, we are one of the smaller guys, who keep the big guns at bay thanks to loyal local customers like you. Do you make the decisions in relation to the purchase of products like ours?

4. **The other guys give me freebies.** Well, everybody loves freebies. I will quote you a clichéd phrase that we have all heard before. *"No such thing as a free lunch."* I will explain why this is 100% correct. Let me share with you a quick story that is actually true. Years ago, a neighbour of mine used to buy a certain brand of coffee every time she went to the store. She bought this brand because it included a gift. It might have been a cup, a spoon or a branded notebook. She was so crazy for the gift that sometimes she would end up spending twice as much as she really wanted, because she was fixated on the freebie and not the purchase. I want you to be obsessed with our product and I believe if you are, your freebie will be the money and time that you save. Then, if you want, you can buy your own gift, and you can choose them too! Are you satisfied that this product can save you time and money?

5. **Not now. I am busy.** I understand and I certainly don't want to bother you when you have so much on your plate. I can call at a more convenient time next week. Could you tell me when would suit you? How about early Monday or Tuesday?

6. **We know the guy working in the other company. He's a friend.** I understand. It is always good to look after your friends. I myself never mix business and pleasure, because if the day comes that I have to make harsh decisions, the last thing I want to do is fall out with a good friend. Think how much more relaxed you would be if you weren't dealing with a friend. You wouldn't have to be walking on eggshells. You could say what you need to say about the product without any qualms. Your relationship with your friend wouldn't be affected. Do you know what makes our service distinctive?

7. **I have been using this product for years and I don't see the need to change.** As the old saying goes: *"if it isn't broke, don't fix it."* I remember the day I moved from using cassettes to CDs. I was always last to change, because there was no need. Although it would take me some time to fast-forward or rewind to the next song, I stuck with it. I didn't see the need for change. Then I realised that everybody else was miles ahead of me when it came to the pleasure of listening to music. The quality of the music was much better on the CD. If I wanted to record different songs from different cassettes onto one cassette, it took time. If I wanted to listen to the very last song on the cassette, I would spend time rewinding and fast forwarding just to get to that point. Now I know that different products and brands are always improving their products and services and sometimes they invent new and exciting products that save time and money. Actually, when digital downloads became popular, I was one of the first to make the leap. I learned that change is good. Can you tell me a bit about your business and what you do here?

8. **You will probably raise your prices once I sign up.** In fact, it is quite the opposite. We reward loyal customers and as part of this reward, we have not raised our prices in the last five years. The only thing that we have raised is the quality of our service and the value that our customers are receiving. Do you know what benefits you will be getting if you use our product today?

9. **I have never heard of you. I will stick with the brand I know.** Of course and it would be crazy of me to even think that you would be interested in something you never heard of, let alone leave the brand that you prefer. But wouldn't it be great to have another option? There are a lot of people in the same boat as you and what they generally do is mix and match. Sometimes they use their preferred brand and other times they use our brand. This has two advantages for you. Number one, you are in control of what you buy and number two, you keep us and the other brand on our toes when it comes to delivering an excellent service and product. Will I put you down for an order, so you can see for yourself?

10. **I am not interested.** Do you know, that's exactly what John from number four said to me the first time I met him. After we explained what we are all about, he gave us a shot. As he says himself, *"It is not a marriage."* That was this time last year and John is still using our product. I am very curious to know why you are not interested. Can you tell me?

Tips and Take Homes

Anticipate your prospect's objections and listen attentively when they are expressing them. Never interrupt the prospect. Always thank the prospect for sharing an objection. This shows that you are interested in their thoughts on your product and their situation.

56. THE DEVIL IS IN THE DETAIL

How it Works

When people are listening to your pitch, it is the concrete details that they are interested in. They want the facts to back up the statements that you make. This is your chance to show prospects that your products can deliver a desired outcome.

What to Do

Sales people will often sell on the facts *i.e.* it is fast, it is green, it is easy. That's not enough. Give more detail. Tell your prospect how fast, how green and how easy. Tell them how they will feel going so fast. Tell them how relaxed they will be looking at the healing green. Tell them how relieved they will be that it is so easy to use. By speaking about the results that one will see by using the product you are addressing a specific problem that your prospect is looking to solve, or a specific goal that the prospect is aiming to achieve.

Tips and Take Homes

Never be vague about the full value that the prospect will get after the use of your products. Prospects want to know the fine points, so give consideration to every aspect of the product, the effect obtained by its use, the timeframe for delivery, the price breakdown, value, strengths and future benefits.

57. DON'T DROP YOUR TROUSERS!

How it Works

Many sales people price match or cut their prices below that of the incumbent or prospective competitor. Don't do this unless it is absolutely necessary and in most cases it isn't.

I remember a prospect that called me up to arrange a meeting when I started with the sales team of The City Bin Co. He told me that he loved the company and the product, but he had one problem. He explained to me that my competitors were giving him a similar service for half the price. He added that if I was willing to match their price, he would sign on the dotted line with me. I scheduled a meeting in his office that afternoon. I was so nervous I wouldn't get the sale that I half decided to not only match the price, but go below the competitor's price.

Before leaving the office, I explained the situation to the Managing Director of The City Bin Co., Niall Killilea. Niall listened to me attentively. When I finished, he gave me the best one-line advice that I have ever received about price matching. He said, *"Oisín, your solution is simple. Show the prospect what makes us different and most importantly, don't drop your trousers'.* He didn't have to say another word. I got it in a nutshell. If you match the price of another product, you are saying that your product is only as good as their product. If you found yourself in a meeting room with your pants down, you would feel pretty silly, wouldn't you? You would feel embarrassed and undervalued. It would be a silly situation. This is exactly what happens when you match or go below the price offered by your competitors.

It is tempting to price match or undercut your price, especially when price is the main motivator for many prospects. Most of the time, it isn't necessary. In fact, when you do it, you are discounting the fact that the value of your product goes beyond price.

What to Do

Rather than pitching your products based on price, sell the benefits of using your products to the prospect. When a prospect objects to your price, sell the fact that you are different. Tell them what they will be missing by not using your product. Show them that like is not being compared with like. Let them know why your products have value and what that exact value is.

My meeting with the prospect was quick and to the point. He asked me to drop my price. I took Niall's advice and explained the difference between the competitors offering and the product I was selling. When I was finished he asked once again for me to match the competitor's price. I said *'No'* and I asked for the business. He gave me a big *"No."* I told him that I respected his decision and wished him well. Two months later, he called me up, saying he was having trouble with the quality of his current supplier's product and signed up with me there and then, at our asking price. After two more months, he was so happy with the excellent service of our company that he converted half his neighbours to using our service. He now tells people who are using our competitors about the positive differences with our product. In his own words, *'You get more bang for your buck.'*

Tips and Take Homes

Be firm in the face of objections about your price. Stick to your guns and if you must move on price, be sure to cut the benefits without compromising the company's name, time and money. Explain that you are not the same as your competitor: you are different and this difference is what makes you better.

58. PEOPLE FOLLOW THE CROWD

How it Works

People love to follow the crowd. They don't like to be left behind. Familiarity is a friend of the prospect and a tool for the sales person. Nobody likes to think that they are missing out on something great. When you are talking to your prospect, you need to tap into that longing for acceptance, to fit in. The more people your prospect knows who are using your product the more likely they are to give it a go. They will want to keep up with their friends and acquaintances.

What to Do

In your conversation with the potential client, tell them the name of someone they know who's already a customer.

'Hey Mike, just to let you know Bob across the way is using our service and Anna from down the road is with us too.'

The idea is to spark their interest and get them thinking that it must be worth looking into. Also, people like to make connections, to feel that products and services are known and recognisable.

Tips and Take Homes

Have a look at your list of prospects and see which ones are from the same area or field of business as your existing customers. Letting the prospect know which neighbour is using your product eases them into a *'Keeping up with the Joneses'* benchmark to follow.

59. DIVERSION METAPHORS

How it Works

Your diversion metaphor is an expression that distracts your prospect and enables you to steer the conversation back to your own products. It will help you resist the urge to agree with your prospect's criticism of your product, which competitor sales representatives may have cited. You can also use diversion metaphors as a friendly way to deal with objections in relation to price.

What to Say

'You know John, it is the difference between the vinyl records that people used to buy and the CDs and mp3s. You have got to move with the times. You know, kids who are 20 years of age today don't know what a vinyl record is and kids born today more than likely won't know what an mp3 download is. My company moves with the times. Are you with me, John?

'Are we comparing apples with apples, or are we comparing apples with oranges? Is it really a good idea to put our product side by side with theirs?'

'To break it down, let me ask you this: If you fly from Paris to New York and you have a choice of taking a balloon, which is the other company, or flying first class on a reliable international airline, which is our company, which would be your first choice, your gut feeling? Which would you feel safest on? And who's going to get you there on time?'

Tips and Take Homes

Diversion metaphors should be kept simple and light hearted. They act as a distraction and an easy way to make or defend comparisons with the competition. You can use them as a confusion strategy to deliver just before closing the sale.

60. TAP INTO EMOTIONS

How it Works

Selling is so such more than a sales script or a product presentation. It is about emotion. If you want to succeed in selling, you need to deliver a pitch that appeals to your prospect's emotions. Logical thinking and powerful selling scripts attract the attention of prospects, but what ultimately buys and sells a product are emotions, because the emotions you evoke give prospects a real connection to your product.

What to Say

Inject a lot of enthusiasm into your pitch, because enthusiasm translates into emotions and it is emotions that will prompt prospects to buy. Look for the good emotions that the product brings out in you and express these emotions. Tap into the things that you love about your product and sell it with feeling and passion. You will trigger emotions in your prospect that will motivate them to buy. People can sense passion and will respond to it. When you sell with genuine feeling, you sell with conviction and prospects will tune into that conviction.

Tips and Take Homes

Connect to your prospect's desires and dreams for your product by being excited. Your prospect will sense your passion. Align your product to the emotional satisfaction it will bring to a prospect. Talk about the relief they will feel after getting a solution to their problem; describe the joy they will feel when they get rid of an existing fear, or the happiness they will feel when they start living their dream; all because of the product you happen to sell. Tapping into the prospect's emotions will enable them to be more open to looking into what you have to offer.

61. ADJUST TO FIT

How it Works

People love when things fit. Round pegs go into round holes and square pegs go into square holes. Pitch your products in a way that demonstrates how they fit your prospect's needs. Sometimes, if you can't find a way to make your product fit you must let go of the fight and move on to the next prospect, who will be a better fit for what you are selling.

What to Do

The fit doesn't have to be perfect. Once there is a need, negotiate to adjust the product to the prospect or sell the benefits that will allow the prospect to adjust to the product.

When your product doesn't meet the needs of the prospect, it is always good to recommend another product or service that would suit them better. This shows sincerity. It tells them you are genuine and leaves the doors of communication open for any future selling with that prospect. There is also the possibility that they will be a perfect fit at a later stage. That's why it is all the more important to plant those seeds of trust and support.

Tips and Take Homes

If there is no fit, use the opportunity to get referrals. They may have a source or database of contacts of potential prospects that could be a good fit for your product.

Create a database with contact details of potential prospects that match well with your product. If a prospect is a non-runner, don't close the door. They may well come back to you at a later date, or know someone who is a perfect fit.

62. SELL THE BENEFITS, NOT THE FEATURES

How it Works

When you are selling a product, it is easy to get excited about all the shiny new features it offers and the cutting technology behind it. The prospect doesn't just want to know how your product works, they want you to demonstrate what results the product will give them and if this will meet and surpass their expectations in relation to what they need.

What to Do

Tell the potential customer exactly what they will gain from your product. Most people buying a car don't want to be burdened with the boring details, the specifications and the size of the engine, unless they are big car enthusiasts. They want to know how comfortable they will feel, how safe they will be, how fast they can go, how much money they can save and how good they will look. Express the personal advantages that they will gain from purchasing your product.

Tips and Take Homes

If you want to know more about the true benefits of your product or service, call 20 of your existing customers and ask them how your products have improved their lives. Also, ask them what the true benefits are for them. This is priceless information that can be used when pitching to your potential clients.

63. LISTEN

How it Works

Sales people love to talk, and they sometimes talk too much. If you don't listen to your prospect, you won't give your best possible pitch. Convincing sales talk is what wins customers over. But talking covers only a small percentage of your pitch. It is when you listen to your potential customer that you really start to sell.

You have one mouth and two ears. That means you need to spend twice as much time listening as you do talking. Give people a chance to discuss their favourite topics. People love to feel they are being heard. If they know you are offering your full attention, they will feel valued.

What to Do

Show the prospect that you are a good listener by repeating back what they say. This demonstrates that you are listening, which in turn proves that you are attentive and the prospect is more likely to trust you. Resist the urge to interrupt the flow of conversation with what you are thinking and feeling. This is their time. Let the prospect talk about themselves and their situation.

Let the prospect do the talking. If the conversation flags, keep the prospect talking by asking simple little questions such as *"Tell me more?"* or *"Can you give me a little background on what you do here?"*

Tips and Take Homes

Control your emotions and opinions at all times when listening to the potential client. Give them an understanding ear in return for their trust. The most important action you can take is to be fully present in the conversation.

64. BE THE EXPERT

How it Works

When you can demonstrate a wide knowledge and understanding of the product you sell, you give yourself permission to be 'the expert'. Prospects like to turn to the expert when looking for information in relation to their situation.

What to Do

Know your product. Know every detail, even if it seems irrelevant. Learn the possible pitfalls that could arise with the use of your product. Know what the benefits and values are for the prospect. Know what your competitors are selling. Know the differences between what they sell and what you sell. Know how much it cost to make your product or to service a client. Know what the marginal profit is on your product or service. If you don't know - ask. Know how much of your product you need to move to be top of the sales team and reach for it.

Tips and Take Homes

As the expert in what you sell, you are always learning. If for some reason you don't know something about your product when a prospect asks, you must never lie. Simply take note and get back on track.

"That's a great question. Let me take note and I will double check with our office for you. I will get back to you before the end of the day with a detailed answer. Does that sound fair enough?"

If you say to a prospect that you will get back to them make sure you do.

65. GIVE OPTIONS

How it Works

Giving options to your potential client means giving them the power to choose. You widen the focus from asking for a simple *'yes'* or *'no'* to giving prospects a choice of X, Y and Z. The prospect will feel more in control when you give them options. They can decide which option is the best fit for them.

What to Do

Change the word "why" to "which." When you use "which," you are giving options. Go to your local supermarket and see how they do it. They have a lower value range, a mid value range and a high value range. These options turn the customer's main question from *"Why would I need this?"* to *"Which one of these will I choose?"* Options create choices and choices help the prospect close the sale themselves. Give the prospect a browsing permit that lets them look without feeling they have to commit. This relaxes the prospect, so they can look at the options that they like, what problem it solves for them, how they think it would make them feel and which price suits them.

Tips and Take Homes

You need to give options to fit different budgets. Showcase the different methods of using your product. Give options to show the various benefits of your product. Offer an incentive for your prospect to go for the top option.

66. USE ACTION PHRASES

How it Works

Action phrases are powerful indirect phases with strong images designed to motivate the prospect into moving forward or making a decision. You show the prospect that you are confident in leading the development of the sale and that you know how to get results.

What to Say

Using action phrases tells the prospect what you want them to do next. Here are some examples of action phrases.

'Hey Joe, let's grab this bull by the horns, what do you say?'

'Steve, why don't we rev up this engine and make some noise. Are you with me?'

'Are you on board, Bob? Then let's fasten the belt and get this plane off the ground.'

Tips and Take Homes

Action phrases are upbeat calls to action that are at their most effective at the end of the meeting. They give you a way to ask the prospect to make a decision without having to spell it out. You will achieve a clear outcome and finish the meeting on a high note.

67. BREAK THE YEAR DOWN TO THE DAY

How it Works

The small numbers are always easier on the ear. Telling your prospect that they will see the benefits in 6 to 8 weeks is better than 2 months. Twelve months sounds better than a year.

When we speak about cost, only €3 or $3 per day is better than €90 or $90 a month. When price is an objection break the year down to the day.

What to Say

Presenting figures like this is a good way to defuse objections about price showing your prospect the affordability of your product from a manageable angle.

'You will start to feel the benefit from using our product, for as little as €2 a week.'

'This option will give you unlimited access to all our products for just €1 a day.'

Tips and Take Homes

Have a look at the overall costs of your product and break them down to the smallest possible denominator.

68. SPREAD THE GOOD WORD

How it Works

Time and time again, word of mouth has been proven to be one of the best forms of publicity, so spread the word! Spread the good word about your products and services. Tell the whole world what you do and what you sell. If you have done your job right, they will know what you sell before they remember your name. If they know your name, but aren't sure what exactly you sell, you need to shout a little louder.

What to Say

Don't be shy about what you are selling. Tell people who don't have any connection to your business about what you sell. Tell your parents, siblings, neighbours and friends. You will be surprised where the next sale might come from.

Tips and Take Homes

To add a personal touch, put a hand written note into every letterbox in your neighbourhood. Introduce yourself, what you do and what you sell. When you are finished delivering to your neighbours, go to the next street and then to the next town. Be the face of your product in your local and surrounding area. People love to buy local.

69. KEEP YOUR PROMISES

How it Works

Making a promise gives a personal assurance to the prospect that you will stick to what you agreed with the prospect. When you keep your promises, you go way up in your potential customer's expectation. You are showing them your commitment to delivering the highest standards of customer service. You will build trust and you will get a reputation for being reliable that will give you the edge over your competitors.

What to Do

If you promise a little extra, give a little extra. If you say to a prospect they will get X, Y, and Z, give them X, Y and Z. If you give a discount on a certain delivery date, stick to it. Write your promises down. Show your prospects you mean business by telling them that you are going to make a note of the actions you have agreed in your diary. Do it in front of them. Recognise that a prospect is under no obligation to keep the promises they made to you.

Tips and Take Homes

Give prospects a timeframe for delivering your promise and stick to it. Never make a promise that you can't keep. If it does happen that a promise slips through the net, be honest, put your hands up and admit the mistake. Promises can be easily forgotten within the chaos of a busy day, so always write down the promises you make.

70. OFFER SOLUTIONS

How it Works

Offering a solution that solves a problem is far more beneficial to the potential customers than just wanting to sell them a product. When presenting a solution to a situation, you must first prove to your prospect that there is a problem that is worth solving.

What to Do

You need to point out the problems and present solutions. Identify the prospect's needs by demonstrating the difficulties and pitfalls with their current situation. Suggest a potential solution and show the value of having the problem fixed as soon as possible. This means that you focus on selling the idea that there is something that needs a solution.

You need to talk more about the cracks and potential holes in their bucket rather than about the product that you know can fix it. If you get them talking about the holes and cracks in their own bucket, they may ask you for a solution.

Tips and Take Homes

Together with the potential client determine the nature of the problem. This is more effective than simply predicting the probability of a problem or likely outcome of a problem that has not yet happened. They must agree with you that a solution is needed and that the solution that you offer will leave them in a better situation than before.

71. BUILD RAPPORT

How it Works

Building rapport with your prospects is fundamental to successful sales. You use rapport to build relationships with your potential client very rapidly. It opens the door to gain their trust, confidence and build long-lasting relationships with your potential client. It is all about getting in sync with your prospect, so that you are singing from the same hymn sheet. When you develop a rapport with someone, you are on the same wavelength. Finding common ground will help you to tap into that wavelength.

What to Do

Start your conversations with a friendly smile. Listen attentively to what the prospect has to say. Look for possible shared interests, dislikes, beliefs, places or circumstances that you can build on. Find common ground and harness any harmony between you and your prospect.

Tips and Take Homes

There are many tools you can use to build rapport, such as mirroring your prospect by matching their body language, their posture and the rhythm of their breathing. Sending gifts or doing small favours without requesting anything in return can give a sense of commitment and strengthen rapport.

72. DO EXACTLY WHAT IT SAYS ON THE TIN

How it Works

This is a great way to build trust among prospects, to prove that what you have said in your pitch is backed up by reality. If you have accurately described the benefits and values of your product, there will be no difference between what the potential customer knows, thinks and sees and what they will actually get.

What to Do

Never over promise and under deliver as this can lead to disappointment. Equally, never under promise and over deliver, as it creates expectations which can lead to disappointment in the future if that same service can't be sustained.

Tips and Take Homes

Always tell the truth about your product: its price, terms and conditions in relation to costs, what the prospect will receive, and when the customer will get their goods. Aim to be realistic in your promises. Make sure what you are selling is the exact same product as the one on the brochure or website.

73. MARKETING:
DOES YOUR MOTHER GET IT?

How it Works

Marketing is a very different skill to selling, yet to get the best result, you need to make use of both. One simple marketing tool that can also be applied to the sales message that you are delivering is to ask: *'Does your Mother get it?'* This is a nugget I picked up from Gene Browne; CEO of The City Bin Co. when he was invited to give a seminar entitled *'How Effectively Are You Retaining Your Customers?'* for The Business Motivation Group in Ireland. Gene, who has won numerous awards in marketing, including 'Marketing Person of the Year' explained that if your mother doesn't get it, nobody will. There are two reasons for this. Firstly, most parents can be our biggest critics. Out of pure love they don't want to see their children fail. Secondly, you are crossing the generation gap and communicating your message to somebody who was brought up with a different viewpoint. In marketing, you identify your target audience; figure out the best ways to reach them, and you place messages where the potential customer can see them. Selling includes everything you do to win and close the sale. You go out to build relationships with prospects, present your product in the best light and influence them to make a purchase. Having the right message for your product will make this path smoother.

What to Do

Work closely with the marketing team to obtain a clear profile of your potential client and understand why they would want to buy your product. Know your product marketing message and who's most receptive to that message. With intense planning and research, the marketers of your business and product decide what product is suited to what target audience. They use marketing messages through advertising and promotions to get information about the product to the potential client. Once there is an interest in the product, you must turn that potential client into a paying customer by using your selling and conversation skills.

Tips and Take Homes

Pitch to your mother! It may sound absurd, laughable and like a hard line to cross, but her feedback will be worth it!

Successful Sales Meetings

To continually win sales on a continuing basis, you must follow a sales process. This is a successful formula that helps you and the sales team manage and move each potential prospect through the sales pipeline, to closing the sale. Having a system with clearly outlined tasks and stages keeps all your activities moving bringing consistency to your selling endeavours.

If you want to have regular successful sales meetings with prospects back to back, plan and schedule your time so you can make the most of opportunities to reach the highest amount of promising prospects and close the most amounts of sales. The more prospects you see, the more sales you will close. Manage your time well by prioritising your tasks so that you can work with a high level of efficiency. Leave no blank spaces in your diary. Ensure that the minimum amount of time, expense, or effort is wasted. If a prospect doesn't show, fill that time with other tasks such as prospect preparation, customer service calls and lead generation activities that will replenish your sales pipeline and give it a healthy outlook.

The most important sales meeting you will attend is not with the prospect, but with your own sales team. This is the meeting where you will set targets, share best practices, review your sales pipeline and provide insights and suggestions to any issues, together with your team. You will give an outline for the day ahead and review of the day gone by. This is the morning huddle, when you and your team take stock, set out your goals and get enthused about what you do. This sets the pace and tone for the meetings with potential customers that follow.

The sales meetings that you have with your potential clients are the backbone of every sales step you take in the process to closing the sale. This is where you talk to the decision makers, with a definite line of action in mind: introducing yourself and your product, building a relationship, delivering your pitch, giving your presentation, asking questions, listening, answering questions and getting an agreed next action to achieve a definite result.

74. THE THREE STAGES OF SELLING

How it Works

There are many systematic approaches and processes to selling a product. Most have three things in common: a beginning, middle, and an end. These can be broken down into three stages.

1. *Lead generating process; information collecting*
2. *Inputting the collected data and making the appointment*
3. *Presenting your product and closing the sale*

A good sales team will have a person dedicated to each stage of the sale where possible. One person is cold calling, with the sole task of making the initial contact and collecting new leads. Another inputs those leads and makes appointments, and the third salesperson is responsible for meeting the prospect, presenting the product and closing the sale.

What to Do

The aim of the first stage is to collect the contact names and details of the person in charge of making purchases; the decision maker. This action takes place face to face and because the sales person is normally cold calling, the point of contact on the day is nearly always the receptionist. You will not do any selling at this stage, but will make an introduction and exchange information. Always keep the initial contact brief and to the point. When you are there, it is very important to do some quick observational work to see which product would best suit the potential client.

'Good morning, my name is Oisín. I am looking for the name of the person who makes decisions in relation to purchasing. Would you have a business card or compliment slip that you could give me?'

After receiving the details, always double check that the name you have is for the person you need to speak to and of course a *'Thank you'* never goes astray.

'That's great. Thank you very much for your time, Have a good day.'

The second stage is all about planning the sale and booking the appointment. Usually you should leave a day or two between the first contact and the phone call to book the appointment. Before calling always check that the details you have are correct. This can generally be done online.

'Hello, my name is Oisín from The City Bin Co. We are currently in your area speaking to your neighbours and would love to call in and speak to Paul for a few short minutes about what exactly we do. When would be good this week to arrange a meeting?'

Always arrange the meetings area by area, so that time is not wasted travelling, searching for places or in traffic.

The third stage is the presentation and close of the sale. This is where you present your product, overcome objections and gain commitment.

It is vital to ensure at the start of a meeting that your prospect is the decision maker and whether they can make a decision one way or the other by the end of the meeting.

'Hello Paul, thank you for taking the time to see me today. Is there anybody else here involved in the purchasing of services and products that should see this presentation?'

This saves you giving the same presentation twice within the one company. The last thing you want is that when you are finished with Paul he says:

'That's great, I love it but I think Bob will have to see it before I can say yes. I never make any decisions without Bob.'

Ensure that the person to whom you are presenting your product is the decision maker and can give you a *'yes'* or a *'no'* before the end of the meeting. You can say at the start of the meeting:

'Paul, Today I will show you my presentation for this product and all I am asking in return is that you commit to letting me know one way or the other if you are interested. Does that seem fair?'

The word *commit* is very significant here, as that is just what you are looking for the prospect to do.

By asking, at the beginning of the meeting, for an answer at the end of the presentation, you are directing the process with a verbal agreement from the prospect. You are indirectly making suggestions to your potential costumer. You are in control.

Tips and Take Homes

Different businesses need distinctive sales procedures to suit their particular sales funnel. The number of stages to have in your sales process depends on your product, industry and resources. Examine the sales cycle of your product from getting a lead to winning the sale. See how many people are involved, how many calls or meetings happen and how many points of contact with the prospect have to be made before completing the sale.

75. ASK QUESTIONS

How it Works

Questions are a salesperson's stock in trade. Always ask questions. An interaction with questions allows the prospect to talk and you to listen. They help you build rapport with your prospect. When people know that you are interested, they will give you the information you need.

What to Do

Tag each part of your pitch with a question to encourage a response and obtain information about your potential client. This allows you to find the best fit for your product and the prospect. Make your questions open ended, so the prospect has to give you a comprehensive answer. Here is a list of guide questions that you can apply to your own product.

- Can you tell me about your business and what exactly you do?
- What aspects of this product most interest you?
- Do you make the purchasing decisions in your company?
- Can you tell me about your decision making process?
- What do you base your decisions on?
- Are you looking at other products in this field?
- Are you speaking to any other suppliers?
- Do you have an idea of what makes our service distinctive?
- Can you make a decision on this today?
- Is it simply this one thing that is stopping you from moving forward?
- Is there anything that I need to explain in more detail to you?
- Have you made any similar changes in the past?
- Are you satisfied that our product can save you time and money?
- What would you need me to tell you that would convince you to buy our product?
- Is there anything else you want to tell me?
- What is a good start date for you?
- What else do we need to discuss?
- What is your expected outcome from changing to our service?
- You seem to be comfortable with changing to our product. Can we discuss a delivery date?
- Can you recommend anyone else who may be interested in what you have heard and seen here today?

Tips and Take Homes

A sales meeting is only really successful if there's a definite outcome. To secure that successful outcome, always finish the meeting with one vital question. At this stage, the prospect will be at their most relaxed, because the meeting is over, so it is the best opportunity for you to make sure that you have covered everything. Simply ask the following:

'I am satisfied that we have covered everything. Is there anything else you would like to know before I leave?'

If you feel you have covered everything, close the sale by asking the prospect if they will do business with you. Ask a closed question that demands a *'yes'* or a *'no'* such as the following:

'John, I am ready to do business today. Is this what you are looking for?'

76. PLAY THE NUMBERS GAME

How it Works

Success in sales is a numbers game. If you want to take full advantage of all opportunities and get excellent results, you need to know how many phone calls to make and how many doors you must knock on to get a prospect. You also need to know how many prospects you will need to schedule to get a customer and how many customers you must win to raise yourself comfortably above your targets.

What to Do

Imagine you and your colleague have the same sales skills, product information and number of leads and work from the same sales script. Now, imagine one difference. Every Monday morning before starting your day you compile a list of 25 extra potential clients that you are going to call that week. It is obvious that you will move more of your product than your colleague. If you are not putting together preparation time at the beginning of each week start doing it now. The rewards will be worth it.

Tips and Take Homes

Write down an above average target that you wish to achieve. Make this list and commit to it. Every Monday morning, before starting your day, compile a list of 25 extra potential clients that you are going to call that week. Give yourself the edge and see your numbers grow by aiming high and landing high.

77. CREATE OPPORTUNITIES

How it Works

Don't wait for opportunity to come knocking on your door. You have to do the knocking. Take responsibility for your own outcomes and look for new opportunities. When you develop the mindset that opportunities are yours for the taking, you will spot them everywhere and you will be in a better position to take advantage of them.

What to Do

If you are selling to businesses, spend one or two days per month driving from one side of your city or town to the other side. Look for new businesses that are getting ready to open. Look for the faces you have never seen before. Talk to these people. Let them know what you are all about.

If you are selling to a domestic market, spend the time to put your name and product information in every letterbox in your area and wherever there is a chance to talk and introduce yourself, do it.

Tips and Take Homes

If no opportunities cross your path, go out and find them. Start with your local newspaper. Every advertisement has the name of a business who is a potential customer. Look at the local groups, clubs and societies around your location. These are all possible melting pots were your potential clients attend. Step out of your comfort zone and network not just in the business community but also through social groups on line and within your area.

78. PLAN YOUR WEEK

How it Works

Creating a really effective weekly plan is a cornerstone of your selling success. Think about what happens when we write a shopping list. More often than not, if we go to the supermarket with a shopping list, we will stick to the list, ticking off the items as we go. We won't allow ourselves to become distracted by items that we don't need.

Planning your week has the same effect. Because you will be on top of your work, important jobs are less likely to fall through the cracks. You won't forget to arrange a meeting or follow through on a lead. As a result, customers will see you as reliable and trustworthy. You will be focusing only on activities that will bring you closer to winning the sale. You will build a dedicated method in your daily routine that will empower you to stay focused on your tasks and targets.

What to Do

Use the shopping-list discipline when you are selling. Write a list of tasks to focus on. When you write things down, you will remember to do them. Decide how much time to devote to each task and what time slot is given to them. For example, start the day with a quick sales meeting to motivate the troops. Block time for client meetings so you are not rushing from one to the other.

Allot time to prospect preparation. This is where you research your prospect so you can build a profile on them and figure out what they need. Taking time to gather this background information will strengthen your sales pitches and bring you closer to a sale. Take time to document the life cycle of the prospect, as it moves through your sales pipeline from initial leads, introductions, meetings, to closing. Make note of how many times you had to call or meet your prospect before they commit to doing business with you. Also, note the time frame of each sale from beginning to end. Collecting this information will give you good indicators for planning future sales meetings. You will get a good idea of how many times you will have to make contact with a prospect and an estimated time period for completion of the sale.

Tips and Take Homes

When you are having a busy week, decide which tasks are most important and prioritise those. Commit to a time frame for completing those tasks. Make short and long term plans. Map out exactly where you need to be, how many prospects you will speak to, who they are, what your intended targets are and stick to them. Revisit and revise you plan regularly.

79. LEAVE NO BLANK SPACES

How it Works

As a busy salesperson, your time is precious. You have got to make every second count. Always fill your appointment book. Leave no blank spaces. If you don't have prospective clients to meet, you can create a to-do list.

What to Do

If you have a cancellation, or a meeting ends early, you can maximise your time by working on your to-do list. Include:

- Cold calls to fellow businesses in the area
- Collect information on potential prospects
- Reconnect with old prospects
- Customer service calls
- Prospect preparation
- Self-motivational and focus exercises
- Seek referrals from existing clients

Tips and Take Homes

Focus on your goal of closing sales, even if you have no meetings set up or you get a cancellation. Fill in the blanks by preparing for your next meeting, looking for new customers to meet, or reconnecting with existing ones. If you do have a cancellation or a prospect that doesn't show up, use the time to contact that person. You can send an email or call and leave a voice mail to re-schedule and confirm another date for a future meeting.

80. MANAGE YOUR TIME

How it Works

When you are selling, your time is important and you need to view it in the same way you view money. Don't be a busy fool, doing jobs that don't bring you towards your end goal of closing the sale. When you do use your time effectively, you will make the most of sales opportunities and you will be on top of your job. Your potential customers will benefit too, because they won't slip through the net when you run out of time. When you are punctual and you are not rushing, you will set the right tone for your meeting. You will be more relaxed and responsive to your prospect. You will show them that you value their time.

What to Do

The first step to managing your time effectively is to monitor your daily activities during a typical week, so that you can create an accurate account of what you actually do. In the course of your work, you may find that there is a lot of distractions. Prospects may ask you to do something for them. Some prospects will want to tell you their life story. You will get caught up in conversation. You will get caught up with your emails and social media. You may get caught up in personal calls. These are all major time takers.

To create reachable targets and goals, concentrate on changing your time management habits by eliminating personal time wasting. Don't take personal calls or get drawn into your personal online social media during working hours. Ask if you are closer to a sale with each task that you do.

Tips and Take Homes

You need to establish routines; regular performance check-ups using organisational systems. Use a simple diary or an online software application. This will allow you to manage your work, plan ahead and add time, as well as taking the stress out of your day. Manage yourself and your appointment diary with efficiency. Stick to your schedule as much as possible.

81. TALK TO THE DECISION MAKERS

How it Works

If you really want to sell, you need to make an impression on the right people. To avoid wasting valuable time, make sure you are speaking to the person who actually has the power to decide whether to buy your products or not. That's the only person who counts. If you are lucky and it is a small business, you will get through to the decision maker right away. But usually, you will be dealing with a receptionist or a more junior person in the company. Be persistent, but not pushy.

What to Say

When you are meeting a contact within the company, double check the responsibility of that person, ask:

"Bill, are you the person who oversees the purchase of products such as what am selling here today?"

'Mary, I just want to make sure I am speaking to the right person. All going well, are you in a position to make a decision on the purchase of this service today?'

'Jenny, is there anybody else that should be at this meeting today?'

Tips and Take Homes

It is critical to understand that the decision makers are normally very busy running their business. If you are not in their diary, they are not going to meet you. To get an appointment, look for an introduction or referral through a third party. Find out if you have any mutual contacts. Don't look for a sale; look for an invitation to meet them. The opportunity for the sale will follow.

82. THE POP SONG MEETING

How it Works

Your sales meetings should be like a good pop song: Upbeat, punchy, lots of rhythm, with three and a half minutes for each member of the team to speak. Pick a time every morning for a pop song meeting. The only people to attend this meeting are the sales team. If you are the only person on the sales team then create and attend this meeting for you.

What to Do

The idea behind this meeting is to give yourself and your team a rhythm. The rhythm and pace is set in the meetings and carries on through the day. Have the meeting at the exact same time every day. Start it on the half-minute and move to the next person three and a half minutes later. Get a stopwatch and commit to the time agreed.

Always start the meeting off with a short good news story. No need for long stories or sad stories. Keep it short, straight and to the point. Speak in bullet points. The agenda of the pop song meeting is to share any blocks or objections you have with prospects. Others in the meeting may have a solution that you can't see. If this is the case the person with the solution can give a quick one-line summary and agree to call the person with the problem after the meeting.

The meeting should also deal with numbers. How many prospects did you call to yesterday? How many did you speak to? How many did you close and win? How many did you close and lose? How many are still open cases? And how many are you going to call today? Sharing this information helps to create healthy competition within the sales team and allows each person to learn from those sales people who are doing well.

A sample programme for the pop song meeting

- *The greatest hits: Short good news sales stories*
- *Any blocks or objections with prospects*
- *Numbers: how many calls, presentations completed, sales closed & won and sales closed & lost*
- *Today's targets and goals*
- *Share ideas*

Go around the room from person to person, taking one topic at a time. At the close of the meeting, share any ideas or visions you may have that will enhance the team or company's goals. Again, keep them short and if they need to be long, you can send a follow up email.

The meeting needs to be moving swiftly. Have your numbers and points written out before you start. When put in practise, the pop song meeting allows the selling machine to move faster. It creates a rhythm within your team that moves every person at the speed of the top performer. Like a good songwriter who keeps writing hits, you will close the sales and reach the targets, especially when there is a rhythm to your step.

Tips and Take Homes

Never go off the format of the pop song meeting. Never change the time of the meeting. There are no excuses or reasons for anybody not to be there. For these meetings, every member of the team must give his commitment to attend. If you can't be there in person, you can phone in and have your call put on speaker.

83. BE HONEST

How it Works

Don't give into the temptation to spin wonderful yarns about your products. Honesty is the only policy when speaking to colleagues, customers and prospects. Prospects are smart and will not be manipulated into buying. Honesty establishes you as a person to trust. Show integrity and genuine understanding for the prospect and their needs. This will be worth its weight in gold whether the prospect signs up to your product or not, because they will recommend you to other people.

What to Say

Stick to the facts and not the fiction when exchanging information. If you don't know something, do not pretend you know. If you don't have an immediate answer, let your prospect know by saying:

'I am not 100% sure on that one. Let me write that down and check it out with my colleague. I will call you before the close of this working day.'

Tips and Take Homes

Let the potential customer know if there is a problem with your product or service and correct these errors. They will appreciate you more for letting them know, telling the truth and taking the steps to fix it. Be upfront about costs, time of product delivery or the likelihood of any other unforeseen detail that the prospect may not notice.

84. GET REFERRALS

How it Works

When you sign up a new customer, you have made the right impression. They clearly think you have something valuable to offer. You can tap into that goodwill and ask them for a referral. They will make great salespeople for your product. Word of mouth is a powerful tool and people will trust a recommendation given to them by friends or associates.

It is not just new customers that can act as salespeople for you. Customers who have been with you for a long time will naturally tell their friends and colleagues about you. These referrals are powerful because they come from people who are loyal to you and know your product inside out.

What to Do

At the end of a conversation, pick your moment to ask for a referral. The prospect might be able to connect you to a friend or neighbour who fits the referral you are seeking.

The more detail you have about what you are looking for the better the chance of receiving referrals. It could be as broad as asking for anybody working in a certain industry, people based in a certain area or the exact name of the relevant person in a particular company that you are looking to meet.

Tips and Take Homes

When you finish conversations with potential customers or clients, never forget to ask:

'Do you know anyone else who might benefit from using these products?'

85. AGREED NEXT ACTION

How it Works

Never leave a prospect without getting an agreed next action. When you get a *'yes'* to your final question, make sure that you and your prospect are clear on what happens next before you leave the meeting. This prevents misunderstandings and confirms your sale.

Depending on where you are in the sales process, your next action will involve establishing the next point of contact or setting a date for implementing the service or delivering the first payment. You can let the prospect decide what that action will be, so they will feel a sense of ownership.

What to Say

Clarify an agreed next action by asking at the end of the meeting for a summary of steps to be taken. The prospect may be very enthusiastic and initiate the next action. If they don't, be ready to prompt them. You can tell the prospect or, even better, they can tell you.

'John, before I leave can we recap on our next agreed step in relation to the implementation of our service so that we are both clear on what is going to happen?'

Tips and Take Homes

Be one step ahead and well prepared by identifying probable outcomes and their specific next steps before the meeting starts. That way, you can deliver a summary of steps to the prospect with confidence. After agreeing on a next action, be sure to put it in your diary. Note the date, time, what is to happen and with whom on your calendar.

86. IT'S OKAY TO WALK AWAY

How it Works

When you sell your product, you will always have a certain percentage of prospects who know how to buy. In the same way that some people become experts at selling, others become experts at buying. They know what buttons to push and which questions to ask to get a discount, or an extra service that is not included in your original offer.

These people are experts in paying below the odds and will go to all lengths to make sure they get the best deal on your product and that you make zero profit. They will tell you that they can get what you are selling cheaper from somebody else.

You are not in a race to the bottom; you have equal power to say *'No'*. You do not want to sell to a person who doesn't appreciate the value of your product. Saying *'no'* to a potential client who is looking to squeeze the juice out of you not only protects the value and benefits of your product, but also tells that person that you believe in what you are selling. When you stand your ground, you will find that a number of these prospects will actually come back to you after experiencing a less than great service from your competitor.

What to Say

You don't need to match the price or go lower to win the sale. When you do this, you are giving all the control over to the buyer. The technique to overcome this is to say *'no'*. Follow your *'no'* with a confusion metaphor, and the values and the benefits of the product you are selling. You could say:

'John, I understand that you are looking for a good deal, but if I was to give you the same prices as the competitors, honestly, I would only be saying that we are only as good as they are and we both know that we are miles ahead in service, value and quality. My grandmother always told me if you buy cheap, you buy twice and you know that is true. Now, if you would like to go with the other company, I will be on my way. However, if you are looking for a product that will do the job and never let you down, here you have it. I say this with total confidence. If I couldn't, I wouldn't."

Or if you preferred to keep it short and to the point you could say:

'Mary, that would be a great deal for you, however a bad deal for my company. I am going to say no on this one.'

Tips and Take Homes

If your prospect consistently tries to work their way out of paying the asking price, remember that you have a responsibility to protect the credibility of your company and the value of your products. Sometimes the right thing to do is to say *'No'* and let your competitors lose money on these guys.

Develop Extraordinary Selling Skills

To develop extraordinary selling skills, you must spend more time with prospects. The more you sell, the more opportunity you have to learn and sharpen your skills. This is one of the key components to becoming a successful sales person. The successful sales person knows that to grow in the world of selling, you have to go out and get your hands dirty. You must have as many selling experiences as possible and learn from every one of them. You must take full responsibility for your role and be accountable for your results.

As a salesperson, you have got to explore every avenue for creating leads and securing sales. It is your responsibility to be branded. Make it easy for the potential customer to know you, like you and contact you. Start equipping yourself with the tools to become a well-rounded salesperson who can rise to any challenge, not just selling the product, but selling yourself. There are lots of extra activities you can do that will boost your profile and draw prospects to you and what you sell.

Leverage the power of referrals and make yourself visible by joining or starting business networking groups. You will generate new ideas and leads. You will build relationships with like-minded professionals. Selling runs on word of mouth.

Create an online presence that will help you strengthen your reputation by communicating with your customers through different sources. Use social media platforms to take ownership of what prospects find when they type key words relating to your industry into online search engine. Start your own sales blog or product user site with instructional videos, tips and reviews.

To be the best, you have to know the best. You need to find the best sales people in the world and learn their secrets. Ask what do they do? How do they do it? Why they do it? Find a mentor that can coach you and push you to new levels.

Give to others what you are looking for yourself. Tell other business owners and managers how much you appreciate their products and services by regularly sending testimonials. If you send a compliment before a pitch, the prospect will be easier to approach.

Leave your prospects with a positive experience of meeting you, the great storyteller, the charmer, the person that they feel they have known for years and the authority figure on the product they are thinking to purchase. Imagine being able to hand your prospect a book that you wrote yourself. A book just like this one, on a topic relevant to their situation and the product you sell. Now, that would be impressive.

87. BUILD YOUR SOCIAL MEDIA PROFILE

How it Works

The best thing about setting up your professional social media presence is that it is free and it is easy to use. You don't need to be a computer genius or Internet savvy to make social media a success. Using these online platforms to boost your image and that of the products you sell demonstrates that you are contemporary. It raises your profile amongst other professionals who might refer your services. It allows you to engage with your clients and prospects by keeping them all in the loop about new offers, products and services. It opens up the possibility for further sales.

It provides a powerful platform that enables you to communicate and catch the attention of potential clients who you may not otherwise capture in the lead generation process.

What to Do

Build a strong web presence to promote yourself as a sales person, as well as the product you sell to add strength to your selling strategy.

Start a weekly or monthly blog giving advice to clients on your product. Talk about who is using your product, exchange tips and tell stories about your customer's experience with the product. This will show potential clients the benefits of signing up with you. Your web presence enables you to give your customers some real time, up to date information, through posts, blogs, videos and pictures.

Create and post videos online which act as an educational toolbox for customers and potential clients teaching them valuable skills about how to get the most from your products. People like to learn and if your online teachings demonstrate your expertise of the products you sell you will attract a new audience.

When you constantly add new content to your social media profiles, you boost your search engine rankings. This gives you online visibility when a potential customer is searching for information about your product. By setting up a social media presence based on your professional identity, you raise your profile to that of a world-class sales person who knows and cares about the customer and the product you sell.

127

Posting nuggets of advice shows prospects that you have a deep interest on the subject that you are talking about. When your prospects research you or your product, make sure they are impressed by the information that they find.

Tips and Take Homes

When you have your different social media outlets up and running let your existing customers know about it. When you are updating the information on the sites, do it at the same time every day if it is daily or the same day every week if it is weekly. People who are following you online will get accustomed to your timetable and tune in.

88. JOIN A BUSINESS NETWORKING GROUP

How it Works

Look for a business-networking group in your area and make it your business to attend. If you can't find one, start one. When I couldn't find a suitable business group, I started a group called the Business Motivation Group, with seven other business professionals. We created a space for business people to share and connect through motivation, support, and personal development. With business motivational speakers presenting a free talk every month, we attract between 30 and 40 members to each meeting. After the presentation the place is always alive with people organically networking. Not only have I picked up new clients from this group, I have developed communication skills, received business mentoring and widened my pool of knowledge when it comes to selling. Business networking groups normally meet weekly or monthly. People from all fields of business come together to build mutually beneficial relationships and exchange leads and referrals with other members. Normally, there is no overlap of business types. A networking group can help you to develop your communication skills. It is a way to win new business and a platform for testing out new ideas and improving your pitch.

What to Do

Join a business-networking group in your area and attend all meetings. Seize the chance to make connections, raise your company's profile, the profile of your product and most importantly, your own professional profile as the number one seller of your product. When you are part of a group, you have access to professional guidance from a range of experts. Follow up is crucial after a business network meeting. Make the most of the opportunities that the group offers by sending group members an email saying how much you enjoyed meeting them. Suggest that it would be a good idea to follow up with them outside the group meetings. Build relationships with fellow members. The payback will be double.

Tips and Take Homes

Use your networking group as a place to brainstorm any problems or objections you may want to sort out. This is extremely helpful, because your colleagues in the networking group aren't biased. They can give you concrete advice from the buyer's perspective.

129

89. FIND A MENTOR

How it Works

The best way to reach the top of your industry is to learn from those who are already there. These people are often incredibly generous with their time and are only too happy to share their years of experience and expertise with up and coming talent.

Mentors are easier to find than you think. You will find them online, through their books and articles, in the business networks you belong to, even among your customers. They are chief executives, business owners, and innovators. They often want to give something back, so why not give them the opportunity.

Finding a mentor is worth more than you can imagine, more than any university can teach you. That's because they will give you a valuable outside perspective. The wisdom they pass on to you will give you the edge in your work and your customers will notice the difference in the improved service you give them.

What to Do

Ask yourself who the top people in your field are, the people you would want to model yourself on. Find their contact details either through your own business network or online. Approach them, indicating that you would greatly value their expertise and that you would like to learn from them. You are not trawling for company secrets; your job is to soak up priceless first-hand knowledge from the experts. You are giving them the opportunity to share the insights that they have gained throughout their career.

Tips and Take Homes

Start tapping into your local network. Find a retired businessperson or respected business owner in your area that has experience under their belt and who wants to give something back. Arrange to meet them for a mentoring session either online or in person, once a month for a year.

90. GIVE TESTIMONIALS

How it Works

You have very little control over the opinions that others have about your service or product, but you have 100% control over what you think of other people's services or products. Asking for testimonials is now standard practise among sales people and business owners, because they give an objective insight into the product that they offer. This kind of unbiased feedback is a valuable boost to a company's reputation. Companies can then publish these glowing reports on their website, adverts, and leaflets.

Sales people who are on the front line play a crucial role in asking for and collecting these testimonials for the products they sell. They know that the opinion of the existing customer is an important tool for attracting potential customers. Extraordinary sales people take testimonials a step further by giving them daily, because they know, in order to receive, you have to give. Your generosity will pay real dividends when the company in question posts your testimonial on their website, including your signature and company logo, which gives you free publicity. Curious prospects and their customers may come to you naturally, without you having to sell.

What to Say

These are examples of testimonials that I have given in the past. No one requested these testimonials. I really did appreciate the service I witnessed from these companies. In some cases, they led to business from the prospect. Remember, it costs nothing to pay a compliment.

To: *'Pura Vida Coffee Shop'*

Hi Rob,

Just a quick note to compliment you on the wonderful atmosphere you have in your coffee shop. I went there twice this week to switch off and have a cup of coffee. Your floor staff are very professional and polite. Well done on creating this gem of a place and I certainly look forward to returning.

Regards,

Oisín Browne,
The City Bin Co.

To: *'Mez's Masquerade'*

Hi Mary,

I have never used your services before, but I want to compliment you after seeing the great job you did on the pirates' costumes at the Pirates of the Caribbean night out last week. I was actually there on the night and I was wowed by the quality and detail of the costumes. When I need a costume, I am certainly going to get it from you. Well done.

Yours sincerely

Oisín Browne,
The City Bin Co.

As it happens, six months later, I had the opportunity to do business with the costume shop when I was looking for somebody to help me design and make a mascot for the company.

Sometimes when it is deserved, it is worth its weight in gold to write an in-depth testimonial. The payback can be worth double the effort put in, as it was when I sent this genuine and heartfelt email to my hypnotherapy trainer after completing a course in Hypnotherapy.

To: *'Bodywatch International School of Hypnosis and Hypnotherapy'*

Hi Niamh,

I am writing to you to express my sincere gratitude and appreciation for a job well done and a course that went beyond all my expectations. The course was of great benefit to me in my role as a sales representative for The City Bin Co. I now find that my communication skills are much sharper. I know how to communicate with my potential client in a more proactive manner and how to suggest the better options to them in relation to our products. Most importantly, I know how to get great results.

This course hasn't just benefited me in terms of my role at The City Bin Co. It has shown me how to easily set up and market my own business, which I have done. Along with working in sales for The City Bin Co, I now run a successful weekend Hypnotherapy clinic called Drop the Monkey Hypnotherapy.

The personal extras were a hidden plus for me. As well as having another skill in my toolbox, my confidence is at an all time high. I thoroughly enjoyed this excellent course and I would highly recommend it to anybody looking for a change in their career, looking for that secret skill that other businesses don't have or simply want a second stream of income.

Regards,

Oisín Browne
The City Bin Co.

Tips and Take Homes

When you enjoy an excellent customer experience, be sure to ask for the manager's email. It is a two-minute job to send a small compliment to a handful of people you interacted with that day. Also, remember that these businesses are potential customers. When you approach a business that you have praised, your testimonial gives you a nice warm way to start your pitch. Gently remind them that you have used their product or service and ask them if they received your email.

91. BECOME A WORLD CLASS STORYTELLER

How it Works

A brilliant way to build up rapport and connect with your prospects is to become a world-class storyteller. Your story doesn't have to be a fantastic Indiana Jones style adventure story, or a highly original tale of genius. It just has to be your own story. Your own story is unique. It is genuine. You need to look for that special feel good story to make a solid connection with your potential clients. Storytelling is the secret ingredient that helps salespeople rise to the top.

Everybody's story is distinctive and personal to them. It sounds so natural and engaging to talk about an event that you have lived through. Because it is your story, it will be easier for you to deliver it with enthusiasm. People love to tell a story, especially when it is their own story and luckily for the sales person, people love to hear a great story. Only you know your story. Only you can tell it.

What to Say

Let me take this opportunity to tell you my own story. I often tell this true short story of how I met my beautiful Spanish wife. One day, my mother asked me to pick up something sweet for the tea. I stopped at a bakery that happened to be on my list of prospects that I wanted to visit. The bakery was packed with customers. There were two girls working behind the counter. I placed my order with one girl and I asked the other for a piece of paper and a pen. I wrote my number down on the piece of paper that she gave me, handed it back to her and told her that I would love to go for a coffee sometime. She called me that night. Five years later, we are married, with two kids and a home of our own.

This isn't just my story. It is a story with a great moral for anyone and especially those in business and selling: *'If you don't ask, you don't get'*. I later found out that it was my wife's first day of work at the bakery. All the staff from the bakery were at our wedding. They made our wedding cake and yes, I signed the bakery up to The City Bin Co.'s services. My wife also knew the power of being a great storyteller. Every day, customers came to the bakery to keep up to date with the on-going love story between the Irish sales man and the Spanish girl working in the bakery.

Tips and Take Homes

Keep your story simple, short and engaging. Let your story grow by telling every single prospect every single day. Remember, they are listening to your story for the first time, so you have the chance to really polish your delivery.

Your story doesn't always have to be about business. Speak about what people love and understand, for example, family, love, kids, and hobbies. Build up a repertoire of different stories that different prospects can relate to. When you tell your story, you are also giving the prospect a chance to tell you their story. This creates a natural human bond, which is all too often missing from the sales process.

92. LEARN TO READ THE ROOM

How it Works

Have you ever walked into a room to meet a prospect and just known before anybody spoke that the atmosphere was full of negativity? Maybe you sensed that your prospects were angry, frustrated or acting out of fear. Or maybe the opposite has happened and you have felt a great sense of energy or mutual magnetism. This is your gut feeling. This is what happens when you tune into your body's reactions and subconsciously read the room. Most of us use our gut instinct when we are buying. It is not always about the facts presented to us; it is how we feel inside about the product that influences our choices.

What to Say

The same applies in selling. Being able to read your prospect's emotional reaction and your own gut feeling is possibly one of the most overlooked, yet easiest skill to master, once you have learned to trust yourself. If you get a strong feeling, act on it by saying:

'Before I continue any further, can I ask you if you are interested in hearing more about this product?'

Tips and Take Homes

Listen to your gut feeling when you are with a prospect. Learn to read how your body is reacting when you are talking to a prospect. If you feel the pitch isn't being received well, it most likely isn't. If you have a gut feeling that the prospect is not interested, then it is likely that they are not interested.

93. PIMP YOUR PROPOSAL

How it Works

A sales proposal is a pitch on paper. A successful proposal must make the prospect want to contact you immediately. In order for this to happen, you have got to pimp your proposal and make it stand out. A proposal will win or lose the sale all by itself. It effectively places you out of the prospect's decision-making process, giving them full control of the buying process without any outside influence. It is a call to action by the prospect to you, saying, *"Here's your one chance to impress me, or I will press the reject this proposal button."*

The best proposals are the paperless proposals. However from time to time a prospect may ask you to send them a proposal, or it may be the only option when you are bidding for a tender. Before you put your valuable time into the preparation of a proposal, you must qualify the sale. If you feel the prospect is only asking for a proposal to brush you off, contact them and ask:

'James, I can have a proposal in your hands first thing tomorrow morning. Before I go and prepare the proposal, can you tell me today that you are interested in learning more about this product? And if I leave the proposal with you, would you be happy for me to drop by next Monday to answer any questions you may have and see if we can do something together?'

Remember, if you are being asked for a proposal, so are your competitors. Therefore, to win the sale you have to stand out and wow the prospect through clear and precise communication, creative thinking and an innovative presentation.

What to Do

Keep away from the run of the mill standard proposal templates. Differentiate your proposal by making it short enough to keep the prospect focused, with rich content that will hold their interest. Put all the meaty information on the first page, including price and an overview of the content of the proposal. Don't have a prospect go looking for the first thing that they are going to want to know. Make it easy for them to find the information. Make sure this information is about the prospect's needs and not your wants.

Give different options of acceptances to encourage a prompt decision. So, if they accept the proposal now, they will receive X, Y and Z on top of the proposed agreement. If they accept in two weeks time they will receive X and Y. And if they choose to leave it until a later undecided date, they get the proposal as it stands. Ask for an acknowledgement of receipt for the proposal and schedule a follow up progress meeting for the soonest date possible.

Tips and Take Homes

Include a personalised video link introducing the prospect to the people that work behind the scenes to create the product. Show your existing clients interacting with your product and the values that they receive from such use. Keep any video you make short and snappy much like a movie trailer. If you don't get the sale, ask for feedback about your proposal. This information is invaluable for strengthening the structure of future proposals.

94. DISPLAY THE BRAND
YOU REPRESENT

How it Works

When you are selling, you are representing a business brand. At every point within the sales process, you have an opportunity to sell your brand to your prospects without even speaking. I drive a branded car. This is the same as having a working billboard advertising what I do every day. It says, *'Hello, I am here and I am opened for business!'*

I love when prospects see me parked and approach me about doing business. I also love to wear The City Bin Co.'s red branded coat over my suit. It looks smart, clean and they have The City Bin Co. logo on the crest. It is comfortable and looks so trendy that prospects often ask me if they can get one. Now, when your prospect is offering to wear your brand before the meeting has started you will know that you are on to a winner.

What to Do

If you drive a car, make sure it is branded so you will be seen. There is no excuse for driving an unbranded car. Why would you sacrifice being seen by all existing customers and future prospects, just so the competitors don't know what you drive or the clients you are going to see? What your competitors see and think is not important; it is what the potential client sees and thinks that is crucial.

If it is raining, bring a branded umbrella and leave it with your prospect. When you are writing down a name or number for a prospect, do it with a branded pen and hand them the pen as a gift.

Tips and Take Homes

If you are working for a bigger company, you can back up the work that the marketing department is doing to build the brand. If you own your business, see yourself as the brand. You must avail of every opportunity to build on your brand. Show your brand. Branding creates a presence and leaves a lasting impression.

95. COMMIT TO A 100 DAY ACTION PLANNER

How it Works

To achieve an objective you need to establish a goal, set targets and create a timeline in which you wish to complete that goal. You can achieve this by committing to an action planner. Your action planner is your vision board. This is a place to tweak your dreams and guide your goals to the materialisation of the results that you desire.

Imagine if you could get a glimpse of where you will be 100 days into the future with any goal or project that you set out to achieve. Maybe your plan is to increase your commission by a certain percentage or you are looking to get a big potential client to sign on the dotted line. Maybe you want to reach a certain level of fitness within a given time frame. Perhaps you would like you see yourself in a more senior role within your team or maybe you would love to start writing the book on your product experience that propels you a step above your competitors. In fact, that's how I started to write this book. I set myself the goal of having the first draft written within 100 days. I noted my progress, what I got done and what needed to be done daily. When that 100-day cycle was completed I started the second 100-day cycle in the project, which brought me right up to having the published book in my hand. When you work on your targets and goals within a focused template you commit to a belief of success and completion. Firstly, you see the goal as it is completed and after, you create the steps to get there allowing 100 days to make it a reality. Committing to an action planner helps you to apply you full effort and concentration to your objective. This creates an unstoppable energy assisting you to cross the line with record results. It will be easier to prioritise important activities and monitor your task completion timeframes.

What to Do

Buy a notebook and start by writing a contract with yourself. In this contract write the result of your end goal, the start date and the completion date, which will be 100 days later. Write down the exact end target as you see it for the particular project or goal you want to achieve. Make it clear and simple. Dedicate a set time frame to the project and stick to it. Finally, sign it and most importantly get a colleague to witness and also sign it.

Write down everything. Be very specific with your targets. Micro-manage the small detail to direct you to the next step. Refer to your planner once in the morning for five minutes to revise the day's most important things to do. Also look at the planner once at the end of the day to write development notes and highlight any potential blockage points. Keep your tasks and actions relevant to the tasks of the day. Don't be jumping three days ahead or dragging your heels on a task from two days ago. Returning to the action planner daily will help you to evaluate the effectiveness of the plan being used. This is a tool that allows you to plan and accomplish your most important tasks on a daily bases.

Tips and Take Homes

Action planners are very effective when working with a team. It allows the team members to align to one collective goal. It holds each individual team member accountable creating an athlete level focus on every task of the day. If it isn't in the action planner, it is not going to bring you closer to your goal.

This is not a diary where you write down your excuses, this is a non-stop action planner that gets you moving in the right direction. Devote a page to everyday.

96. GIVE OUT YOUR BUSINESS CARDS

How it Works

A business card is a great way to introduce yourself to a prospect. When you hand them out at the start of the meeting, you are introducing the possibility that you will do business together.

It is the action of giving the card that is important here. You immediately take control of your pitch by making an indirect suggestion. Giving out your business card opens up your prospect to the idea of receiving.

What to Do

Make a habit of using your business cards. Don't worry about what the prospect will do with them. It is what you do with them that matters. It is your calling card and the potential client can't call you if they don't have your details.

Introduce yourself as you hand out your card. It will strengthen the prospect's memory of you.

'Hello John, I am Oisín from The City Bin Co. Before I begin, let me give you my business card.'

Tips and Take Homes

Carry your business cards with you at all times. Have a stock of them in your briefcase, wallet or bag, so you won't miss an opportunity to hand them out. Attach them to your product, or to a brochure or flyer. Give two or three to each prospect and ask them to pass them on. Make sure your details are clear and accurate, so prospects will have no trouble contacting you.

97. WRITE A BOOK

How it Works

Books are the new business cards. They tell a prospect who you are and what you stand for. They give you the edge over your competitors. Is the prospect going to call the sales person who sells bells, or the sales person who sells bells and wrote the book called *'Get the Best out of your Bells'*. There is an awe factor, where a prospect will be delighted to be associated with the expert. From a buyer's perspective, you will be seen as an authority on the subject of what you are selling. You are the author of a book on that subject. Investing time in a writing project is fun and it also gives you an opportunity to learn, as your motivations for selling your particular product will become clearer to you. You will be able to explain yourself more effectively to your prospects and that will reap endless awards.

What to Do

Writing a book is much easier than you think. Start with a title, and then write the contents page. Create a structure for each chapter and then flesh it out. You don't have to write a novel. A small *"how to use X"* or *"the guide to getting the best from X"* booklet can work. You don't have to look for a publisher either. There are a lot of online *'print on demand'* printing companies who specialise in small print runs.

Tips and Take Homes

There isn't a single aspect of life or work that you can't write about. Whether you sell paint, candles, or insurance or if you are a mechanic, an accountant or a vet, every product and any service can be written about. Find the angle that's a good fit for you. If your prospect is interested in the product, they will be interested in your book. Even if the prospect is not interested in the product, reading about how it works may whet their appetite.

Books make great gifts for prospects. For new prospects, it is a gentle introduction to the product. They are a great add-on product for existing customers. When you give a prospect a business card, there is a danger that the card will go out of sight, into a wallet or into a bin. Books are left on tables or shelves, where other people can pick them up and read them. This gives you new opportunities.

98. IDENTIFY THE INFLUENCERS

How it Works

It is not always possible to reach the decision makers immediately when selling your product. However, if you can identify influencers associated with the decision maker, their circle of friends or business, you may open a direct channel that will bring you a step closer to meeting the right people. These are the guys who know you, know what you sell, have used your product, love your product and would recommend it. They are already singing praises about your product. This is word of mouth at its best. The opinions of these influencers are valuable to you and the decision maker. They may already have a trust relationship and rapport built with the prospect. You will find several influencers within any one sale that can help you promote your product to the right person.

What to Do

Research and identify the influencers by looking at your existing customers and their connection to potential prospects. Create opportunities to speak to them. Make contacts and build relationships with influencers. Find out if they already have an established connection of trust with the prospect. Look for the influencers within the prospect's circle. The gatekeepers, the caretakers, the cashiers, the assistants, the neighbours, the receptionist, other suppliers, and even the bin men, are all examples of possible influencers who can persuade the decision makers to make a purchase. You can ask them for an introduction when and if the time is right: *'John, I would love to meet the purchasing manager for your store, would it be possible for you to arrange that for me?'*

Tips and Take Homes

Understand that the power that influencers have in any business or community largely depends on the size, culture and relationship structure within that area. Connect with influencers, not to make the sale, but to encourage them to send the right praises in the right direction. Don't sell to influencers, as they are more than likely already fans of your product. Build rapport, keep connected and create outlets such as social media pages, leaflet drops and advertising that gives them a platform to tell your story.

99. VISUALISE SUCCESS

How it Works

Allow yourself to be over the moon about getting a sale before you even get it! This is how visualisation works. When you visualise the end result of your sale, you recreate a vision in your mind of how you desire the outcome. Visualisation prepares you for the real moment, changing your dreams and goals into reality. It enables you to relax and be comfortable in the actual sales environment, as you have lived through the situation in your mind. You create a familiarity with a future event that has yet to happen. Professional athletes use visualisation techniques to train their mind, so that when they are actually competing in their area, it feels like they have done it many times before.

What to Do

Find a quiet space where you can close your eyes and spend five minutes with your imagination. Clearly define your goal and the end result you wish to achieve. See the desired outcome in your mind. Don't just imagine it, feel the emotions that you would have with that outcome. Replay every part of the meeting with the prospect. The greeting, the small talk, presenting the product, the prospect's desire for your product, the environment, the smiles, the detail of the conversation and the firm closing handshake. Practice visualisation on a daily basis to get in a positive frame of mind and align your thoughts with what will happen. You must believe the movie in your mind to succeed. If you can make it happen in your head you can make it happen in reality.

Tips and Take Homes

Before you start visualisation, close your eyes. Take three deep breaths and let go of all the tension in your mind and in your body. A good time to practice is first thing in the morning, when the mind is quiet or last thing before you go to bed when you are starting to switch off from the waking world. When coming out of a visualisation session, allow time to connect with the real world. You can do this by repeating the technique of taking three deep breaths and letting go. With each breath, allow your eyes to open and make yourself fully alert and aware of your surroundings.

100. LEARN LESSONS

How it Works

The more you learn from your interactions with potential customers, the more you will improve your skills. Nothing beats the lessons you learn from real life experience. You may have been to college, read sales books, browsed through websites, yet with every sale, there is a lesson you can learn. Make an effort to better yourself every time.

What to Do

Be willing to fail and to learn from failing. Learn from your prospects, customers and from your work colleagues. Always fine-tune your tactics, in the same way a professional singer never stops training their voice. Whether you win or lose a sale, don't be afraid to ask your prospects what influenced their decision. Then incorporate their feedback when you are planning your next sale.

Tips and Take Homes

Back up your sales experience with professional sales books, sales courses or Internet tools that can teach you the latest techniques. Don't just read them, put them into practice. Take the best bits and mould them to suit you. Exchange tips and techniques with work colleagues.

Be willing to see the lesson in every sale. If you really want to learn valuable lessons ask yourself the following two questions of every encounter you have when interacting with people in the business world, no matter what final outcome materialises:

1. Who is the teacher?
2. What is my lesson?

Bonus Chapter
Meet the Mentors: Interviews with top selling teams, business owners & business consultants

Imagine for a moment that you have the opportunity to meet with top sales teams, business owners and business consultants from many successful companies. They each give you great tips and suggestions based on their experiences and successes. I interviewed people who work for highly successful businesses, from small businesses that offer very personal, one on one customer service to large corporations that are leaders in their respective field. These businesses operate in different industries and countries allowing you to incorporate lessons from their sectors and cultures into your own. I asked everybody the same three questions and the answers I got were very different, but there was a common thread through all of them. The word "listen" came up a lot. They also agreed that you should keep your pitch short, simple and quick. Above all, the answers were raw and honest. They have made all the mistakes and they want to prevent other people from going down the same road. This makes their advice very beneficial to anybody wishing to improve their selling techniques.

Learn how the best sales people and businesses place a high importance on understanding the customer's needs. They are consistently asking the right questions and listening attentively to the answers. They are not afraid to ask for the sale and not afraid to ask for more. They are focused on results. They manage their time with methodical accuracy, allowing them to take advantage of an above average number of opportunities, prospects and customers. Excellence and customer service are essential components in their product. Building rapport and establishing professional relationships with people from a wide range of businesses, cultures and traditions comes naturally to them. They know that to be the master of their destiny, they must always be tuned into their winner's mindset. If you want to be great at selling, you have got to learn from the best. Time spent being mentored enables you to get very important real life information from experts who have travelled a similar path in selling and have succeeded. The tips you pick up from tapping into a mentor's know-how and resources can be as valuable as a three-year business course. Meeting mentors gives you access to real-world experiences. They will guide you to understand your needs within the selling arena while helping you to avoid the pitfalls they have already encountered in their selling career.

Meet The City Bin Co.

Name:	James Kent
Title:	Sales Manager
Company:	The City Bin Co.
Location:	Ireland

The City Bin Co. has an ethos of providing excellent customer service and a mission to be the global service leaders in the waste industry. The City Bin Co. has been a winner of the Deloitte 'Best Managed Companies (Ireland) Award' in 2009, 2010, 2011 and a 'Gold Standard' winner in 2012.

Question 1: *What are your top selling words?*

- Value
- Options
- Reliable
- Benefits

- Improvement
- Results
- Trust
- Customer

- Solution
- Different
- Service
- Agree

Question 2: *What are your top tips for selling?*

- Always look for a **next agreed action**
- Demonstrate that what you are offering is **different**
- Always go back to the **benefits**
- Give multiple **options**

Question 3: *What is your advice to somebody starting a career in selling?*

- **Listen** before speaking
- Dress to impress. **Be presentable** and **be prepared**
- Stick to your strategies and don't over promise
- **Qualify** at every stage

Meet HubSpot

Name:	John Marcus III
Title:	Outbound Sales Manager
Company:	HubSpot
Location:	Massachusetts, United States of America

HubSpot is an inbound marketing software company that helps businesses transform their marketing from outbound lead generation to inbound lead generation enabling them to "get found" by more potential customers in the natural course of the way they shop and learn. HubSpot has won over 50 marketing awards and has over 7,500 paying customers.

Question 1: *What are your top selling words?*

Who, where, what, when, why and how.

The sales process is highly consultative, so understanding a prospects need is the number one priority when closing a sale.

Question 2: *What are your top tips for selling?*

Be **curious**. Focus first on the issue your prospect is trying to solve, and then look into ways your solution might help. Trying to pitch a product without understanding business pain is like throwing spaghetti at a wall and hoping something sticks.

Question 3: *What is your advice to somebody starting a career in selling?*

Start as close to the front line as possible. Cold calling is a great start (if you are right out of college) or working with a transactional sale are two ways to get exposure. If you get multiple times "at bat" you stand a much better chance making more mistakes and learning faster.

Meet 1-800-GOT-JUNK?

Name:	Brian Scudamore,
Title:	Founder and CEO
Company:	1-800-GOT-JUNK?
Location:	Vancouver, Canada

1-800-GOT-JUNK? is the world's largest junk removal franchise with 200+ Franchise Partners throughout the United States, Canada, and Australia. Brian Scudamore has built a company that has a reputation for excellence and customer service. The company has become know as the 'FedEx' of the Junk removal industry.

Question 1: *What are your top selling words?*

- Partnership
- Solution
- Value

Question 2: *What is your top tip for selling?*

Understand your business and your customer's business inside out; this way you will exude **confidence** and ability, which will earn your customers **trust** and their business.

Question 3: *What is your advice to somebody starting a career in selling?*

Incorporate your own personality into your sales process. Part of what your customer is buying into is **YOU** and if you are not genuine, they may not see you as a real person or someone they can trust.

Meet Cobone

Name:	Paul Kenny
Title:	Founder and CEO
Company:	Cobone
Location:	Dubai, United Arab Emirates

Cobone.com is the number one group buying website in the Middle East and throughout Africa offering group coupons for products and services. Paul Kenny, CEO & Founder of Cobone won the Middle East Entrepreneur of the Year Award in 2012.

Question 1: *What are your top selling words?*

- Enthusiasm
- Trust
- Belief
- Clarity
- Win-Win

Question 2: *What is your top tip for selling?*

Adapt your selling style to the client and always try and **understand** their point of view and deliver a proposal based on that. Always be **creative**!

Question 3: *What is your advice to somebody starting a career in selling?*

Practice with your friends, try selling old clothes or anything that you might have. You will realise early in your career that if you gain people's **trust** easily you can definitely be a great sales person.

Meet Breosla

Name:	Paul Fallon
Title:	Sales Consultant
Company:	Breosla
Location:	Colorado, United States of America

Breosla is a business acceleration firm that improves how clients create, deliver and retain value by investing at the early stages of growth with active participation in business model, process and execution. Paul Fallon's sales success is focused on cultivating new business and ensuring existing account retention.

Question 1: *What are your top selling words?*

- **Pain** - Why are we here today?
- **Decision** -Who is involved in making decisions?
- **Effect** - Who else does it have an effect on?
- **Time** - Does this fall in line with your budgeting?

Question 2: *What are your top tips for selling?*

- **Listen** twice as much as you speak
- Build a **solution** for your prospect based on what they need
- Think like the executive team
- Bring the future to the present

Question 3: *What is your advice to somebody starting a career in selling?*

Volume, Volume, and Volume: If you work harder, make more calls, visit more prospects, and start more trials you will close more deals, make more money, build a bigger network, learn more and advance your career.

Meet Fyffes

Name:	Gerry Cunningham
Title:	Managing Director
Company:	Fyffes
Location:	Ireland

Fyffes sell to the sellers and are the worlds leading importer and distributor of tropical produce with operations in Europe, the US and Central and South America, headquartered in Dublin, Ireland.

Question 1: *What are your top selling words?*

- Be **efficient**
- Be **cost effective**
- Be **competitive**
- Best **service**
- Best **brand**
- Be **reliable**

Question 2: *What is your top tip for selling?*

- **Know your business** inside out.

Question 3: *What is your advice to somebody starting a career in selling?*

- **Listen** and **Learn**
- Don't be afraid to **question**
- Always **follow up**

Meet Alondra Music S.L.

Name:	Jesus Varas
Title:	Founder
Company:	Alondra Music S.L.
Location:	Madrid, Spain

Alondra Music is Spain's leading independent sub-publishing company who focus their energy on representing foreign catalogues and placing songs of established artists together with products and television adverts.

Question 1: *What are your top selling words?*

- Always say **thank you**
- Have **respect**
- Treat the client as you wish to be treated.

Question 2: *What are your top tips for selling?*

- **Be polite** and do not pester people
- Do not speak ill of your competition
- There is no such thing as failure, only **experience**

Question 3: *What is your advice to somebody starting a career in selling?*

- When you go to work, leave your personal problems at home
- Good manners opens doors
- Whatever you do, do it well

Meet Da Tang Noodle House

Name:	Catherine O' Brien
Title:	Owner
Company:	Da Tang Noodle House
Location:	Galway, Ireland

Catherine owns and runs the famous northern Chinese 'Da Tang Noodle House' based in the west of Ireland. Catherine believes that repeat sales come when you enrich the customer's experience with an authentic welcoming service and product.

Question 1: *What are your top selling words?*

- **Confidence** in your service and clients
- **Nourish** your clients
- Have **consistency**

Question 2: *What are your top tips for selling?*

- **Engage** with your customer
- Be open, **friendly**, warm and relaxed

Question 3: *What is your advice to somebody starting a career in selling?*

- Apply **quality** to every aspect of what you sell
- Be **passionate** about your service
- Take ownership of what you do
- Take pride in what you sell

Meet Aroa's Flowers

Name:	Aroa Rubiano
Title:	Owner & Florist
Company:	Aroa's Flowers
Location:	Milan, Italy

True to her logo's tagline, *'Aroa's Flowers, made with love'*, Aroa brings a unique international experience to her selling. This has brought her to work on the frontline of the best florists from the west of Ireland to the busy city of Barcelona before setting up her successful shop in the heart of Milan.

Question 1: *What are your top selling words?*

- Demonstrate **professionalism**
- Be **competent**
- Serve with **kindness**

Question 2: *What are your top tips for selling?*

- Offer something **different**
- Give a great **service**
- Know your products

Question 3: *What is your advice to somebody starting a career in selling?*

- Always be **positive** and **polite**
- **Invest time** in studying your business area
- Sell **quality** products

Meet Ginuine and Renaissance brands BV

Name:	Neil Everitt
Title:	Chairman
Company:	Ginuine Ltd and Renaissance Brands BV
Location:	Switzerland

Neil Everitt is chairman of independent spirits companies Ginuine Ltd and Renaissance Brands BV, and SARE, a leading developer of residential Real Estate in India. Neil's career focuses on growth, development and leadership.

Question 1: *What are your top selling words?*

- You
- Better
- Feel

Question 2: *What are your top tips for selling?*

- Walk in the other person's shoes
- Sell benefits, not features
- Take the long view. You don't need to win every battle/every point on the deal

Question 3: *What is your advice to somebody starting a career in selling?*

- The best sales people are those who are best at being themselves
- The product/service is secondary
- People like buying from people

Meet Alpha Private Equity

Name:	Nicolas Macquin
Title:	Partner
Company:	Alpha Private Equity
Location:	France

Nicolas is an expert in corporate finance and private equity. As a partner in Alpha Private Equity, a pan-European private equity fund he invests in mid-market LBOs and growth capital transactions across continental Europe.

Question 1: *What are your top selling words?*

- Quality
- Pleasure
- **Value** for Money

Question 2: *What are your top tips for selling?*

Firstly, obtain the word *'yes'* three consecutive times from the person you want to sell something to and secondly, create a favourable environment.

Question 3: *What is your advice to somebody starting a career in selling?*

Know your customer as well as yourself, so you can leverage on your personal strengths as a sales person. Always **think long-term**, as if a bigger sale was to happen next.

Meet RTC Holdings SA

Name:	Octavian Radu
Title:	Founder
Company:	RTC Holding SA,
Location:	Romania

Under the leadership of Octavian who has an experience of over 20 years in a wide spectrum of businesses from finance, cars, mobiles, book shops, cafes, furniture stores to brewery and investment, RTC holdings have grown to be one of the biggest employers in Romania.

Question 1: *What are your top selling words?*

- Win-win
- Partnership

Question 2: *What are your top tips for selling?*

Understand the needs of the people sitting next to you. Not necessary the 'customer's needs', but the 'buyer's needs'. Not only their financial needs, but what would make them happy.

Question 3: *What is your advice to somebody starting a career in selling?*

Selling is a job where you will meet a lot of different types of buyers. Learn to understand their needs, and your success will be substantial.

Meet ICSS S.A.

Name:	Anastasios Economou
Title:	Vice President
Company:	ICSS S.A.
Location:	Greece

Anastasios is Vice President and Managing Director at ICSS S.A., a specialized aviation service provider. Leading in the field of sales, purchases of aircraft, airplane management, the emphasis for Anastasios is on better customer service to drive better sales.

Question 1: *What are your top selling words?*

- Only
- Value

Question 2: *What are your top tips for selling?*

Listen to what your prospect is saying and then, adopt your offering to what you have heard.

Question 3: *What is your advice to somebody starting a career in selling?*

- Be **patient**
- Always **listen**

You have a lot to learn from people, even people who drive you crazy. Human behaviour is very complex and selling really exposes you to many of its facets.

Meet E-Carbon SA

Name:	Frederic Gerken
Title:	President
Company:	E-Carbon SA
Location:	Brussels, Belgium

Frederic Gerken, President at E-Carbon SA, a global alliance of privately held electrical carbon product manufacturers is dedicated to maximizing customer satisfaction.

Question 1: *What are your top selling words?*

Customer is king and there's no small customer.

Question 2: *What are your top tips for selling?*

Listen more than you speak. Selling is 20% product related and 80% relationship and time.

Question 3: *What is your advice to somebody starting a career in selling?*

The customers are the best teachers about your products. You will learn most from them. Spend the maximum possible time on the road visiting them and as little time as possible on internal meetings.

Customers enjoy meeting new people who have something valuable to say, so, it is up to you to rise to their expectations.

Meet Voucherry

Name:	Ammar Charani
Title:	Chairman
Company:	Voucherry
Location:	United States of America

Ammar Charani heads up Voucherry, an online platform connecting cause supporters with merchants, and generating contributions to charities making Voucherry a great sales, marketing, rewards & retention tool for companies.

Question 1: *What are your top selling words?*

- Don't you think so?

Question 2: *What are your top tips for selling?*

- Tell me, don't sell me.

Question 3: *What is your advice to somebody starting a career in selling?*

Put yourself in the place of the buyer and ask:

- What is in it for me?
- Do I need this now?

Meet Maxol

Name:	Des McGovern
Title:	Area Sales Manager
Company:	Maxol Limited
Location:	Dublin, Ireland

On the back end of a selling career that has continued unbroken for over 35 years in various markets which includes hardware supplies, tobacco, electronic cable and oil, Des McGovern is the area sales manager for Maxol, Ireland's oldest and foremost independent oil company.

Question 1: *What are your top selling words?*

- Yes
- Service
- Commitment
- Trust

Question 2: *What are your top tips for selling?*

- Always **ask questions**
- Give **options**
- **Ask** for the sale – sometimes it is as simple as that
- **Competitive edge** – the competitor's weakness is your strength

Question 3: *What is your advice to somebody starting a career in selling?*

- Be **honest**
- **Listen** before you answer
- Ensure you are speaking to the **decision maker**
- **Persevere** – an extra call or visit can seal the deal
- Be **punctual** and always be **presentable**
- Always show **gratitude**

Meet Peter F Doyle & Co.

Name:	Peter Doyle
Title:	Founder & Director
Company:	Peter F Doyle & Co.
Location:	Ireland

Peter worked in a variety of financial and non-financial roles in electronics manufacturing for 25 years before concentrating on business consultancy and accountancy.

Question 1: *What are your top selling words?*

- Service
- Service
- Service

Question 2: *What are your top tips for selling?*

- Know your customer and the service they need
- **KISS** – Keep it simple stupid
- Take the pain out of the service you are offering
- **Make it easy** for the buyer to see what you are offering by avoiding jargon

Question 3: *What is your advice to somebody starting a career in selling?*

- **Know what you are selling** inside out. If it is a product, then use it and be familiar with it. If it is a service then try it out.
- **Know your customer** and tailor your presentation for their needs, their size and capacity to work with you

Meet Retail Dynamics

Name:	Christo Popov
Title:	Founder and CEO
Company:	Retail Dynamics
Location:	Bulgaria

Retail Dynamics focuses on producing and promoting healthy food and beverages as well as educating consumers on the role of food for health and overall wellbeing. Following a career with Shell and McKinsey, Christo Popov became a serial entrepreneur with projects in consumer goods and retail, focusing on innovation and new market developments.

Question 1: *What are your top selling words?*

- If I... Would you...
- Do I understand correctly?
- Please tell me more…

Question 2: *What are your top tips for selling?*

- Make the prospect talk
- Make the prospect say **'yes'** a number of times
- **Listen**
- Never make a firm proposal – always start with if…
- *'No'* is just the start of the discussion

Question 3: *What is your advice to somebody starting a career in selling?*

- You do not have to be a chatterbox or extrovert to succeed
- You cannot overlook the experience that comes with **practice**
- **Understanding** people and the "*feel*" for the deal is key

Meet Meterlogix

Name:	Ollie Walsh
Title:	Managing Director
Company:	Meterlogix
Location:	Ireland

Ollie has been very successful in obtaining global contracts for his products. Meterlogix is dedicated to reducing the energy consumption of businesses by monitoring areas of waste energy output.

Question 1: *What are your top selling words?*

Listen: Your customers know their business much better than you do. Listen to what they have to say, as they know what they need. Once they tell you what it is they need, you can then fulfil it. Feedback from my customers tells me that I have listened to them, not talked over them telling them my opinions without even knowing what problem they need solved.

Act: Making the sale is not the end of the process. If you expect to retain the client, you must act to make sure you deliver your promises.

Follow up: Actively look for feedback or follow up information from your customer, good and bad. This is part of the process of continuous improvement for you, the sales person.

Question 2: *What are your top tips for selling?*

Have a positive and confident attitude at all times. Your attitude has a dramatic effect on the client and the possibility of a sale.

Question 3: *What is your advice to somebody starting a career in selling?*

Know your product/service inside out, but if you are caught out with a question you can't answer, do not wing it. It's okay not to know everything and your customer will appreciate you getting them the correct answer as opposed to the result if you guess it wrong!

Meet RTE Radio

Name:	Antony Whittall
Title:	Commercial Director
Company:	RTE Radio
Location:	Dublin, Ireland

As part of the Irish national public broadcaster, RTÉ Radio incorporates public service, talk, news, current affairs, sport, documentary, drama, arts, music and entertainment. 1.3 million listeners tune into RTÉ Radio every week and the station broadcasts 10 of the most popular radio programmes nationally.

Question 1: *What are your top selling words?*

- Tenacity
- Dexterity
- Clarity
- Mutuality

Question 2: *What are your top tips for selling?*

It's about winning **hearts** and **minds**. You need to do both.

Question 3: *What is your advice to somebody starting a career in selling?*

You can go under, around and over a wall.

Meet Creva

Name:	Noel Kelly
Title:	CEO
Company:	Creva
Location:	Ireland

An honours graduate from Smurfit School of Business in Sales Management, Noel has taken his company Creva to the international arena with clients across Europe, USA, Canada, Middle East and Russia.

Question 1: *What are your top selling words?*

- **Follow up**
- Be of **service**
- Make partnerships work
- Selling is stories

Question 2: *What are your top tips for selling?*

Know that a customer buys from a person NOT a product.
Build **relationships** and a reliable **reputation**.

Question 3: *What is your advice to somebody starting a career in selling?*

Surround yourself with great sales people and learn from them. Know your customers as well as you should know your products. Be clear about your sales goals/objectives.

Meet Cloud Consulting Ltd.

Name:	Tim Pullen
Title:	Managing Director
Company:	Cloud Consulting Ltd.
Location:	Ireland

Tim is a sales and delivery focused business director with extensive experience of building and leading successful teams. Supplying technical and business project resources, Cloud Consulting Ltd. are one of Ireland's leading cloud technology consultancies.

Question 1: *What are your top selling words?*

- **Yes**

Question 2: *What are your top tips for selling?*

- **Listen**
- **Qualify** hard
- Never over sell
- **Understand** your customer's business
- Develop **trust** based selling
- No surprises – ever

Question 3: *What is your advice to somebody starting a career in selling?*

- Don't sweat the small things
- **Learn** when not to sell
- Always try and work with the best people you possibly can
- Be **honest**
- Have **fun**
- Follow the money

Meet PC Pitstop

Name:	Stephen Connolly
Title:	Owner
Company:	PC Pitstop
Location:	Galway, Ireland

PC Pitstop looks after the IT requirements for SME's across Ireland. Stephen Connolly gives additional support with his selling skills, broad knowledge and troubleshooting skills within the IT industry.

Question 1: *What are your top selling words?*

- I **understand** your **needs**
- Be **prepared**
- Be **genuine**
- Develop **trust**
- Eliminate the word 'No' from your vocabulary
- Encourage the word 'Yes'

Question 2: *What are your top tips for selling?*

- Always go the extra mile
- Selling is not finished until the Customer has left with a smile and paid in full
- First impressions make lasting impressions
- Smile & be friendly

Question 3: *What is your advice to somebody starting a career in selling?*

- Be persistent, but not pushy
- Motivate yourself – do what it takes to get into the zone
- Learn to love your phone – make calls & follow up
- Understand the difference that the margins make to the bottom line

Acknowledgments

Firstly, I would like to give a big thank you to my beautiful wife Eva who has displayed pure love and a lot of patience while I was stuck to my laptop day and night writing and rewriting this book. You are my mentor in love, life and family. Thank you to my family. My mother Margaret, my father Ray, brothers: Ronan, Parisch and Gene. Thank you to my children, Mani and Alana. You are my mentors.

To all The City Bin Co. staff and customers who have interacted with me over the years, thank you. You are my mentors. A special big thank you to Gene Browne, CEO of The City Bin Co. (and my brother!) for his endless support and belief in me and in my ideas. You are my mentor.

Thank you to all the members and co-founders of the Business Motivation Group who have inspired me to reach for the stars. You all are my mentors.

Thank you James Kent, Niall Killilea, Declan Varley, Catherine O Brien, David Keane, Ollie Walsh, Peter Doyle, Paul Nicell, Maricka Burke Keogh, Josef Hrehorow, Evy Perez, Diarmaid Mulcahy and Mairead Heagney for your guidance and support in business and life. You are my mentors. A special thank you to Ray Walsh for pre ordering the first two copies of this book before I had even put pen to paper.

Thank you to my editorial team led by Derbhile Dromey of Writewords. Thank you for the conversations filled with editorial direction. Anthony Sloan, thank you for sharing so much of your valued time and generosity in reading, rereading, editing the first drafts and sharing stories of times gone by. Patrick Donohoe of Hume Brophy, thank you for your professional feedback and input. You are my mentors.

To Niamh Flynn, director of Bodywatch ltd, International School of Hypnotherapy and Hypnosis. Thank you for teaching me a great skill that compliments everything that I put my hands to in life, the coffee meetings and for encouraging me to go with the selling idea. You are my mentor.

Thank you Dr. Paddi Lund for writing the beautiful foreword for this book and for sharing the extra tip. You are my mentor. Thank you Verne Harnish, Marshall Goldsmith, Libby Gill, Al Ries, Steve Schiffman and Jeffrey J.Fox for taking a huge leap of faith and endorsing my book before it went to print. You are all leading experts in the world of business motivation and leadership guidance. You are my mentors.

About the Author

Oisín Browne has worked in sales and marketing for more than twenty years. During that time, he has sold everything from paintings, Spanish Christmas carols to waste and recycling products. He has worked at The City Bin Co.'s headquarters in Ireland since 1998.

Oisín is a contributor to the business section of the biggest newspaper in the west of Ireland 'The Galway Advertiser' with his fortnightly 'Drop the Monkey Business' column, sharing business nuggets & life inspirations.

In 2011 Oisín co-founded the Business Motivation Group, a business support group that offers motivational talks, support, and inspirations.

When he's not too busy selling and learning, Oisín enjoys travelling with his family between his home in the west of Ireland and the north of Spain, where he immerses himself in the rich Galician and Spanish culture.

www.oisinbrowne.com